Organizational Learning

Organizational Learning

The competitive advantage of the future

Gilbert J. B. Probst

and

Bettina S. T. Büchel

Prentice Hall

London   New York   Toronto   Sydney   Tokyo   Singapore
Madrid   Mexico City   Munich   Paris

Originally published in German as
Organisationales Lernen
by Dr. Gabler Verlag in 1994
© Betriebswirtschaftlicher Verlag
Dr. Th. Gabler GmbH, Wiesbaden 1994.
Editor: Barbara Marks

First published in English in 1997 by
Prentice Hall Europe
Campus 400, Maylands Avenue
Hemel Hempstead
Hertfordshire, HP2 7EZ
A division of
Simon & Schuster International Group

© Prentice Hall Europe, 1997

Typeset in 10/12 pt Century Schoolbook
by MHL Typesetting Ltd, Coventry

Printed and bound in Great Britain by
T.J. International Ltd

Library of Congress Cataloging-in-Publication Data

Probst, Gilbert.
    [Organisationales Lernen. English]
    Organizational learning : the competitive advantage of the future
/ Gilbert J.B. Probst and Bettina S.T. Büchel.
       p.   cm.
    "Originally published in German as 'Organisationales Lernen' by
Der Gabler Verlag in 1994."
    Includes bibliographical references and index.
    ISBN 0-13-462326-6
    1. Organizational learning.   I. Büchel, Bettina.   II. Title.
HD58.82.P7613   1997
658.4'06--dc20
                                         96-41863
                                       CIP

British Library Cataloguing in Publication Data

A catalogue record for this book is available from
the British Library

ISBN: 0-13-462326-6

---

1 2 3 4 5   01 00 99 98 97

Contents

Preface   *ix*
Introduction   *xi*

1 The importance of organizational learning   1

1 Management systems under review   *1*
2 Globalizing tendencies, growth and redimensioning   *3*
3 Growth of knowledge   *4*
4 The importance of time   *5*
5 Changing values   *6*
CASE STUDY 1: ABB — the logic of global business   *10*
WORKSHEET I: Assessment of learning needs   *12*

2 What is organizational learning?   14

1 Definition of organizational learning   *15*
2 Difference between individual and organizational learning   *15*
3 Theories of action   *20*
   3.1 Official theories of action, or espoused theories   *22*
   3.2 Theories in use   *22*
4 How we recognize organizational learning   *23*
CASE STUDY 2: Jakob Schläpfer Ltd   *26*
WORKSHEET II: Analysis of organization's store of knowledge   *30*

3   What is the nature of organizational learning?   **32**

1   Adaptive learning   *32*
2   Reconstructive learning   *33*
3   Process learning   *35*
CASE STUDY 3: Organizational learning at departmental level: the training department in ABB   *38*
CASE STUDY 4: Organizational learning at institutional level: the restructuring of Digital Equipment (Europe)   *40*
WORKSHEET III: Analysis of forms of learning   *42*

4   What triggers learning in organizations?   **44**

1   Learning through turbulence and crises   *44*
2   Learning as a result of slack   *46*
CASE STUDY 5: IBM   *48*
CASE STUDY 6: Hewlett-Packard   *49*
WORKSHEET IV: Analysis of factors which trigger learning   *53*

5   Who are the agents of organizational learning?   **55**

1   Individuals as agents   *55*
2   Elites as agents   *57*
3   Groups as agents   *57*
4   Social systems as agents   *58*
CASE STUDY 7: Group project in Allianz Insurance   *60*
WORKSHEET V: Record of critical agents of learning process   *63*

6   What are the barriers to learning?   **64**

1   The difficulty of unlearning   *64*
2   Obstacles to unlearning   *66*
  2.1   Organizational defensive patterns   *66*
    2.1.1   Skilled incompetence   *67*
    2.1.2   Defensive routines   *68*
    2.1.3   Fancy footwork and malaise   *69*
  2.2   Norms, privileges and taboos as barriers to learning   *70*
  2.3   Information disorders   *71*
CASE STUDY 8: The Challenger disaster   *73*
WORKSHEET VI: Force field analysis   *75*

7   Facilitating organizational learning   **78**

  1   Learning profile of the organization   *78*
  WORKSHEET VII: Learning profile   *82*
  2   Initiation of learning processes   *84*

8   Learning by developing a strategy   87

  1   The strategic context   *87*
  2   Games in microworlds   *88*
  EXAMPLE: Business games   *89*
  CASE STUDY 9: Tanaland   *90*
  CASE STUDY 10: Use of a microworld in a company planning seminar   *93*
  3   Scenario technique   *95*
  EXAMPLE: Strategic environment scenarios   *96*
  CASE STUDY 11: Kuoni Travel Group   *98*
  CASE STUDY 12: Royal Dutch Petroleum/Shell   *102*
  4   Strategic control   *103*
  EXAMPLE: Meaurement systems   *105*
  CASE STUDY 13: Skandia AFS   *105*

9   Learning by developing a structure   **108**

  1   The structural context   *108*
  2   Projects as a form of organization   *109*
  EXAMPLE: Project management   *110*
  CASE STUDY 14: Winterthur Insurances   *113*
  3   Network organizations   *116*
  EXAMPLE: Heterarchy   *117*
  CASE STUDY 15: Forbo International   *119*
  CASE STUDY 16: McDonalds   *121*
  4   Forms of cooperative arrangement   *122*
  EXAMPLE: Strategic alliances   *123*
  CASE STUDY 17: Digital Equipment Enterprise   *126*

10   Learning by developing a culture   **129**

  1   The cultural context   *129*
  2   Development of vision and mission statements   *130*
  EXAMPLE: Vision and mission statements   *131*
  CASE STUDY 18: Swisscontrol   *133*

CASE STUDY 19: Gore & Associates Inc.   *137*
3   Communication fora   *138*
EXAMPLE: Analysis of assumptions   *139*
CASE STUDY 20: Volkswagen Ltd   *140*
4   Company climate   *141*
EXAMPLE: The image analysis   *142*
CASE STUDY 21: Hewlett-Packard Ltd   *144*

11   Learning by developing human resources   **147**

1   The human resource context   *147*
2   Learning partnerships   *148*
EXAMPLE: Human resource development alliances   *149*
CASE STUDY 22: Digital Equipment Corporation   *150*
3   On-the-job interventions   *151*
EXAMPLE: Learning-oriented project work   *152*
CASE STUDY 23: Oticon Holding A/S   *154*
CASE STUDY 24: British Aerospace Plc   *156*
4   Maps   *157*
EXAMPLE: Mapping   *159*
CASE STUDY 25: ABB Industrie Ltd   *159*
CASE STUDY 26: Aare-Emmenkanal Ltd   *162*
CASE STUDY 27: Hoffmann–La Roche   *162*

12   From knowledge to ability to the intention to learn   **166**

1   Definitions of learning   *166*
2   Knowledge: instruments for learning   *167*
3   Ability: can we make learning happen?   *168*
4   Intention: the will to learn   *169*
5   Maturity of the organization   *169*
6   The building block principle   *173*

Bibliography   *175*
Further reading   *180*
Index   *185*

Preface

Are some organizations more intelligent than others? Can organizations learn and change? Intuitively, we easily accept that organizations are able to increase their capacity for action and change. Practically, this is more difficult to understand. Yet, organizational learning is more than just a metaphor.

Back in the late 1980s, Gilbert Probst gained experience about learning in a large US company, Clark Equipment. In this company, individuals had understood the need for change, were ready for it and knew what action to take: but the whole did not change in the 'expected' way. This company is not, however, an exception. Some companies use early warning signals and are thus ready for learning; others wait until a crisis emerges. What we noticed was a wide range of different learning styles and triggers within companies.

After several years of experience in industry and teaching in the field of systems theory, organizational design and business strategy, organizational learning became our prime topic of interest and determined our research activities. When Gilbert Probst first taught a course on learning organizations long before this book was under consideration, it was not clear what these organizations looked like and which instruments supported and facilitated learning. It was the Swiss Association of Organizational Design that asked us to research learning and write up the theoretical background and practical experience. This was the beginning of our fruitful and challenging collaboration. We are continuing to work together on different topics related to learning, such as using cooperative arrangements as 'learning tools'. The topic of learning has lead us to look for tools in the area of knowledge management which might facilitate learning.

The book is an overview of organizational learning. Cases are provided to illustrate learning companies and the difficulties in applying such an approach. Last but not least, the book has been designed to propose the use of management tools for a productive discussion of learning processes. We are looking forward to a lively dialogue.

We wish to thank the companies that gave us the chance to work with them and provided us with the 'learning' information for the cases in this book. We also wish to thank Steffen Raub for patiently reading the text several times. Finally, we wish to acknowledge Anne Thomas for her excellent work in translating this book from German into English.

Geneva, 1997   *Gilbert Probst and Bettina Büchel*

Introduction

The concept of organizational learning has achieved prominence amongst the ideas which now influence management studies. We should be wary of dismissing it as the latest fad, since the topic of learning is attracting increasing attention both in academic circles and in business practice. One of the main reasons for this is the increasing pressure of change on companies as they move towards the close of the twentieth century. The rate of change accelerates steadily, and companies must find their bearings in an increasingly complex environment. The ability to learn is thus of paramount importance. Companies which do not successfully implement organizational changes, and which fail to cultivate their potential to develop, may soon find themselves amongst the losers. In future, according to de Geus (1988), learning will be the only lasting competitive advantage.

The concept of organizational learning has aroused a great deal of interest. Unfortunately, considerable confusion attaches to the definition and use of the term. It is easy to see that organizations need to be able to learn in order to maintain or increase their competitiveness. It is more difficult to arrive at a concrete definition of organizational learning, and to differentiate it from learning by individuals. These two kinds of learning are quite distinct. If we confuse them, we make the common error of trying to deduce from a part the properties of the whole.

There is a dearth of analyses of how organizational learning can best be understood, and how the process can be initiated and maintained. We hope that this book will go some way towards filling the gap. The first six chapters of the book look at the conceptual framework of learning. We do not attempt a comparative description of current theories; we have chosen instead to look at the nature of organizational learning processes by analyzing the determinants of learning. We then go on in Chapters 7–11 to discuss ways in which management can shape learning. We consider how managerial guidance in the areas of strategic management, organizational design, culture and human resource management can precipitate and strengthen learning processes. We focus not so much on individual instruments as on their process-based application and their effectiveness in promoting learning or in overcoming obstacles to it.

1

The importance of organizational learning

1 Management systems under review

We live in a world of accelerating change. People are pushed — or push themselves — towards ever higher levels of achievement. The pressure on social systems grows steadily. Business and social systems are interrelated, and people are confronted every day by complexity and novelty. They have to cope not only with an increasing number of tasks but also with open dynamic processes and changing parameters. This calls into question the content and meaning of the basic dimensions of our society, such as school, work and family, and the role and significance both of social systems and of individuals. Thoughtless pressure to accelerate growth will very soon lead to social problems which cannot be ignored. We therefore need to develop a new approach to the evaluation of business and management systems.

Drawing on the ideas of Humberto Maturana, Schmidt (1991) offers the following formulation of the need for new paradigms: 'all institutions which subordinate one person to another must be eliminated; all institutions must be orientated towards satisfying biological needs and cultural aims; we must increase our understanding of the relationship between biological existence and ecological stability; we must improve our insight into the plasticity of societies which are non-hierarchical, and, as such, are highly artificial, man-made systems'. Organizational learning offers an alternative paradigm by which systems can change, thus permitting us to redefine the economy and society (Figure 1).

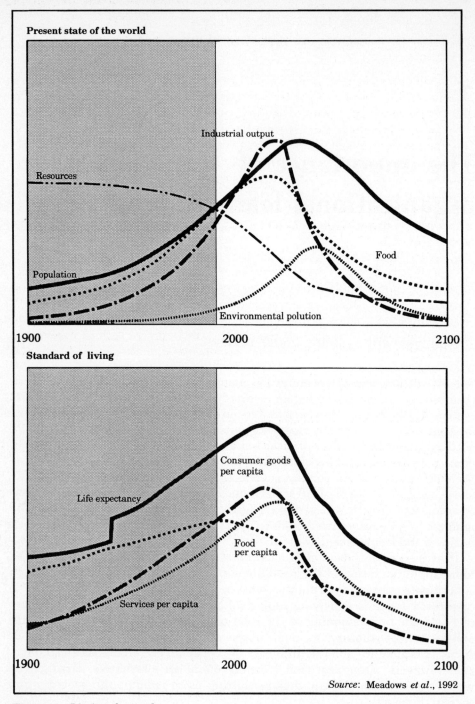

Present state of the world

Industrial output

Resources

Food

Population

Environmental polution

1900   2000   2100

Standard of living

Consumer goods
per capita

Life expectancy

Food
per capita

Services per capita

1900   2000   2100

Source: Meadows *et al.*, 1992

Figure 1   Limits of growth.

2 Globalizing tendencies, growth and redimensioning

Economic pressures such as growth and profit — the yardsticks of our economic system — force institutions to be increasingly competitive. In response to the demand for increasing growth, firms conquer new markets, and thus increase their market presence. This has resulted in the globalizing tendencies which have been apparent for some time. More and more companies are trying to have a finger in every pie. Previously, increasing the company's critical mass by the pursuit of unlimited growth was seen as the path of the future. Various forms of cooperation, such as strategic alliances, joint ventures, and mergers and acquisitions have become important because they offer companies a way of maintaining competitiveness by increasing their size in different parts of the world (Figure 2).

Competitive pressure has implications not only for the size of enterprises but also for their structure. They may have to consider redimensioning, particularly in times of crisis. This raises the question of what measures an organization should adopt to attain its optimal size. The current preoccupation with redimensioning is reflected in the frequent use of the terms 'downsizing' and 'rightsizing'. We may conclude that ways are being sought of controlling globalizing tendencies, taking into account both internal and external circumstances.

At the same time there has been a progressive shift of emphasis in

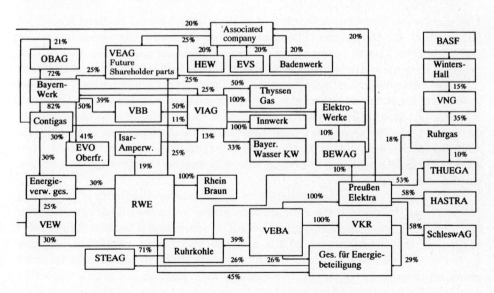

Source: M&A Review Database, Hoppenstedt, 1992

Figure 2 Cooperation in the German gas and electricity industries.

management from quantity to quality. Companies are recognizing that resources are limited, that bottlenecks may occur and that there are limits on the progress to be achieved through growth. Aspects of quality which have recently been considered include a company's problem-solving ability and capacity for action. These aspects will continue to be of vital importance because new ways of looking at problems call for increased flexibility both now and in the future. This means that companies must look for new ways of improving their future capacity for action, and their problem-solving ability.

Our times are characterized by a preoccupation with quantitative growth, which at present drives the development of the economy. In the future, we shall have to look for different dimensions which can offer new values within a framework of successive changes, or which can generate a new paradigm. It will not be enough to look to growth spurts as a way of raising critical mass; we shall have to look beyond this, to find potential for qualitative growth. It is clear in retrospect that qualitative growth has played a subordinate role up to now. Companies have therefore been unable to achieve the competence in problem-solving which they needed for global development. The ability to meet external circumstances by building up internal capacities for action is a critical factor, and is central to the topic of organizational learning.

3 Growth of knowledge

The increasing interconnectedness of economic and social systems has major implications for the future. The expansion of the knowledge base in society and in institutions is becoming more important. One reason for this is that existing structures are extremely complex, so it is difficult to understand their internal interdependencies. To cope with all this complexity, we need increasing amounts of knowledge on which to base our decisions. However, the constant state of structural change means that it is not sufficient simply to go on adding to the knowledge base; there must also be a process of adaptation, so that existing knowledge is constantly re-examined and restructured. New situations must always be analyzed; this will lead to the development of new management skills.

In 1972 the Club of Rome published its first report on the limits of growth. In this report, it pointed out the dangers of technical and scientific progress, and of the increasing loss of human control over it: modern man is increasingly unable to foresee the consequences of his actions. The report painted a negative scenario of the state of the world, and drew attention to the threats faced by mankind (Figure 1). However, the authors also pointed out man's unlimited potential for learning, which could yet be exploited to combat this dismal state of affairs. Learning is the process of preparing for new situations, so that future problems can be overcome (Peccei, 1979).

Pautzke (1989) stated that 'Careful cultivation of the capacity to learn in the broadest sense, i.e. the capacity both to acquire knowledge and to develop practical abilities, seems to offer a realistic way of tackling the pressing problems of our time' (p.2). The problem-solving skills which have developed up to the present have proved inadequate to solve our political, economic and social problems. Whilst admitting the importance of the quantitative aspect of learning (increasing the knowledge base by adding to it), we must recognize that the qualitative aspects (developing skills for the future, or differentiating the store of knowledge) may be even more significant in the future.

4 The importance of time

Time has become a decisive factor in competition. We are confronted by constant progress, ever-shortening innovation cycles and overlapping political changes. If we look at the competitiveness of different countries, we see that it is sometimes impossible to make up for missed opportunities (*World Competitiveness Report*, 1992) (Figure 3).

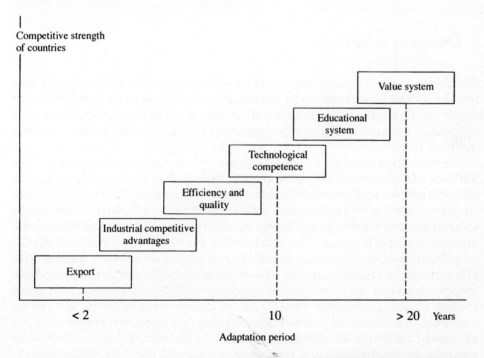

Source: based on *World Competitiveness Report*, 1992

Figure 3 The significance of delays for the competitiveness of different countries.

There is no adequate treatment in the literature of the time factor as a resource, or of how to manage it. This is surprising because timing is a vital consideration when new products are being launched, or decisions being made on investment, disinvestment or setting up new enterprises or joint ventures. Timing is often the variable which determines success or failure. A report from Arthur D. Little has shown that a delay of six months in launching a product can mean a devastating loss of profit. It can pay to launch the product earlier, even if this means higher development costs (Figure 4).

Percy Barnevik, the chief executive officer of Asea Brown Boveri (ABB), has put this last point as follows: 'Why emphasize speed over precision? Because the costs of delay exceed the costs of mistakes' (Taylor, 1991). In ABB, the stress placed on the time factor is more than mere lip-service: it has been incorporated into the management of the company (see Figure 6 in Case Study 1). Comparative studies have shown a previously unimaginable shortening of innovation cycles; this means that reaction times in management must be shorter than can be achieved using traditional structures, processes and methods. It is clear that new methods must be found which take account of the changing significance of the time factor.

5 Changing values

In a changing environment, institutions are under constant pressure to find new solutions which will preserve future competitiveness. The difficulty of surviving within the existing economic system and the principles on which it operates is compounded by uncertainty about the future, and constant changes in values (Figure 5).

Rapid changes in values frequently produce potential for conflict. As a result business ethics come under increasing scrutiny. Every job applicant has to consider aspects of the company's identity (what company shall I work for, what does it do, what is its environmental policy?). Working life, with its attendant obligations and values, is changing; similarly, social structures have come under increasing pressure. The accelerating pace of change, higher levels of uncertainty and the increasing complexity of value systems have become part of society and its institutions. In view of the uncertainty of the future, and the changes in society, we must mobilize tomorrow's intellectual resources. It is not enough to adopt a passive stance and let change happen to us. We see an increasing readiness to replace the existing management system and its associated values by an alternative system. In the past, change was brought about by external crises (new technologies, changed political circumstances, globalization). Today we see, both in society and in organizations, not just a readiness for change but a positive will for change. In other words, we are

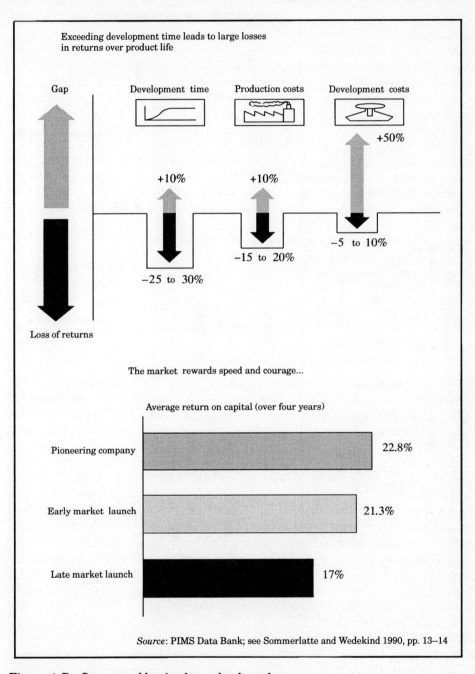

Figure 4 Profits secured by timely market launch.

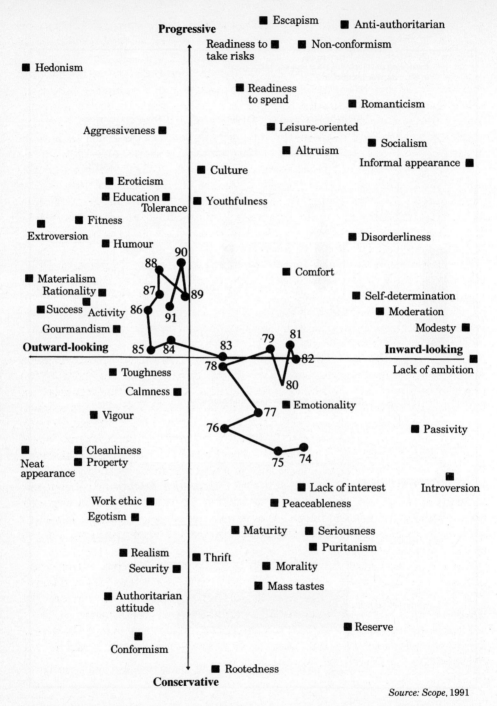

Figure 5 Changing values: psychological map of Switzerland for the period 1974–91.

Source: Scope, 1991

moving from a *reactive* attitude to change to a *proactive* attitude. The will for change implies a need for new management principles and provides the foundation for a new approach.

If social systems want to be able to cope with change and to master new and complex problems, they must adapt and think ahead of developments. Change takes the forms of new discoveries, new technologies and political changes, as well as of new structures which evolve within the organization itself. Learning processes must go beyond simple quantitative increase of the competence of an organization. Surface adaptations are not enough: learning must involve the underlying structure of the organization and bring general changes in codes and philosophies. In other words, learning affects the culture of the organization. The culture has an implicit influence on learning and action: it may facilitate, or it may hinder. In our study of learning, therefore, we shall be looking not at quantitative growth but at qualitative changes in structures, processes and rule systems within companies.

In recent years, companies such as Digital Equipment Corporation, IBM, Hewlett-Packard and ABB have restructured and have integrated new acquisitions into the main company. As a result, they have undergone changes in structure and in internal values. These companies are therefore good examples of learning organizations and will be used for purposes of illustration in the discussions that follow.

In the search for new management principles, there are three key criteria which lead to success: *responsiveness* to the needs of the members of the organization who will be affected; the *learning capacity* of the organization, and the organization's *capacity for action* (Pautzke, 1989). The capacity to learn could be the critical resource of the future; indeed, it is often critical already. Careful fostering of the capacity to learn is the only realistic way to tackle present problems. Social systems such as profit and non-profit organizations in the political, administrative, economic and social spheres *need* to be able to learn; efforts are being made to ensure that they *will* be. Their survival depends, amongst other things, on the ability to learn as an organization. The capacity for institutional learning, in the sense of gaining knowledge which increases action potential and the ability to solve problems, is considered in more detail in the rest of this book.

How can organizations make sure that they will survive within their environment, that they will change, and, most importantly, that they will learn? The approach which we describe shows how companies can acquire the qualities they need to move successfully into the twenty-first century.

Organizations must acquire the necessary capacity for action in their various fields of operation. The first step is to develop a learning model of the organization which will assist in this process.

Case study 1

ABB — the logic of the global business

Asea Brown Boveri (ABB) is a Swedish/ Swiss industrial enterprise and a world leader in producing equipment for power stations, power transmission and transport. It is also active in other areas of industry. In 1993, it was an international, decentralized company employing 214,000 people in 1,300 firms in 140 countries.

Following the merger of Brown Boveri Company (BBC) and Asea, and the consequent increase in complexity, the company was faced with a need to redefine its management systems. The following principles were adopted.

■ Think global, act local

Given the globalizing tendencies and the growth of the company, this was a key principle which needed to be established in different areas of the business and in different countries.

■ Restructure all parts of the company across the world as profit, service or cost centres

To support this restructuring, and to facilitate the exchange of information between units, the growth and broadening of the knowledge base was made a priority.

■ Increase management competence through global networks

The merging of two culturally and historically disparate enterprises, and the changes which this brought to the company and its values, meant that ABB had to work hard on company identity. Uncertainty about the future made this even more necessary.

■ Define ABB's vision and mission statement and its basic values, emphasizing customer focus[1]

In the face of the difficulties described above, ABB had to learn to cope with change. The company had to meet the demands of a changing environment while carrying out internal reforms and processes of differentiation; this meant that it had to learn *quickly*. It would not otherwise be in a position to master future developments.

The fact that ABB underwent a successful learning experience does not mean that it now has no further need to learn. Learning is a continuous process. If it is neglected or abandoned, the results can be catastrophic. Furthermore, organizations do not learn overnight; they need a great deal of time to digest and live with new arrangements of the kind described. The various companies which constitute ABB act within their own markets and their own specific environments. To remain competitive, they must continually improve their operational efficiency and customer orientation. At the same time, they are joined together in a network; they depend on each other, and serve the same customers or order from the same suppliers. They must therefore learn to deal as a global organization with customers and suppliers in ways specific to ABB; they must speak the same language on matters such as quality and timing, and project the same

---

[1] Other basic values of ABB are: presentation of the company as a unified group, high standards in business ethics, 'employees are our main capital', high quality, protection of the environment, quick action.

values. Learning processes of this kind can be supported and accelerated by a variety of instruments which redefine the management system, such as customer focus, process management, time-based management, quality management, acquisition management and so on. The interaction of the new management methods is now a source of further learning within ABB.

Figure 6 shows how the integration of time-based management (TBM), total quality management (TQM) and supply management (SM), together with customer focus provide a basis for high operational efficiency at ABB.

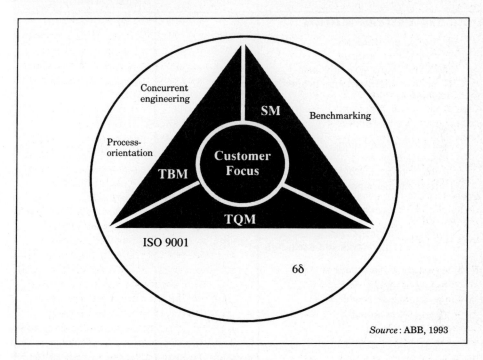

Source: ABB, 1993

Figure 6 High operational efficiency at ABB.

WORKSHEET I		
Assessment of learning needs		
	In what area is there already a need for learning?	Where might there be a need for learning in the future?
Key factors	Past triggers of learning	Possible future triggers of learning
1. Analysis of external factors		
Ecological environment – Availability of energy – Availability of raw materials – Trends in environmental protection – Recycling –		
Technology – Production technology – Product innovation – Substitution technology – Information technology –		
Economy – International trade – Balance of payments and exchange rates – Inflation – Capital markets – Employment – Tendency to invest –		
Demographic and sociopsychological trends – Population trends – Work mentality – Tendency to save – Leisure behaviour – Attitude towards automation – Culture –		
Politics and law – International conflicts – Party political developments – Economic policy – Social legislation and industrial law – Significance of trade unions – Freedom of enterprise –		

WORKSHEET I (continued)		
Key factors	**Past triggers**	**Possible future triggers**
2. Internal company analysis		
General company development – Turnover – Cash flow/profits – Costs –		
Marketing – Market performance – Prices – Distribution – Communication –		
Production		
Research and development		
Finance – Capital – Liquidity –		
Personnel – Deployment – Team spirit – Company culture		
Capacity for innovation		
Know-how – Purchasing – Cooperative arrangements – Holdings – Acquisitions –		
Strategy – Strategic positioning – Increase in value –		

2

What is organizational learning?

Current approaches to organizational learning are manifold and include both a pragmatic and theoretical discussion of the topic. The existence of a multiplicity of definitions is therefore not surprising. The traditional psychological approach to learning focuses on learning by individuals. Psychologists belonging to the classical conditioning and behaviourist traditions describe learning as the acquisition of chains of reactions which persist over time. They attribute changes in behaviour in given situations to repeated experience of those situations. Most of their findings are based on the study of observable behaviour. Learning theory is therefore concerned with observable behaviour, and neglects the cognitive processes of the individual.

There is, however, an alternative psychological approach which, unlike classical learning theory, concentrates on mental processes and cognitive interactions with the environment. In the course of these interactions, individuals create their own representation of their environment, based on experience, expectations and beliefs, and on previously developed cognitive patterns. The approach centres on changes in potential behaviours and in underlying cognitive structures (Bandura, 1979). This theoretical approach is better placed to explain how new behaviours arise. It offers a second point of departure for the study of organizational learning.

If the cognitive approach is adopted at the individual level, the learning potential is a function of a person's insight, cognitive abilities, intelligence and experience. Experiences are moulded by socially transmitted skills, motivational history, interests and value judgements. These factors exercise a strong influence on a person's learning ability and, together with the difficulty of the material to be learned, they determine progress in learning.

Most psychological definitions of learning remain at the level of learning by the *individual*. Systems theoreticians take a different approach: they are concerned not so much with individual learning processes as with the system or organization as a whole. From this point of view, learning by an organization can be seen as the satisfaction of the needs of a collective. The primary focus of attention is the organization as a framework for individual action. Most analysts who approach organizational learning from this angle give prominence in their theories to *interactions between the individual and the organization* (Argyris and Schön, 1978; Morgan, 1986; Hedberg, 1981; Pautzke, 1989).

1 Definition of organizational learning

We define organizational learning as follows:

> **Organizational learning is the process by which the organization's knowledge and value base changes, leading to improved problem-solving ability and capacity for action.**

The ability of individuals to learn is not in dispute. It is much more difficult to understand how organizations as a whole can learn. An organization consists of individuals, and, in the final analysis, they must be the ones who learn. Although the relationship between learning at the organizational level and learning by individuals is not fully understood, one can say that learning by individuals is a prerequisite of organizational learning. Thus, the members of the organization are the real point of departure. Through their own frames of reference, they learn for the company.

2 Difference between individual and organizational learning

There is as yet no comprehensive and integrated theory of organizational learning. There are, however, some approaches which have a certain originality, even though they depend to some extent on theories of individual learning. The distinction between individual learning and organizational learning can be made in terms of knowledge which does not depend on particular members of the organization, as in the following example:

It is the duty of an employee in the payroll department of the fictitious firm

Optics Ltd to produce a statement of salaries at the end of every month. This statement is produced according to certain rules laid down by management. Through trial and error, the employee arrives at an optimal procedure. If this procedure is documented and followed, the organization has gained knowledge which exists independently of the individual. If such knowledge is stored in systems within the organization, *capacity for action* is abstracted, and the knowledge becomes replicable. This increases the basic store of knowledge of the organization, and the additional knowledge becomes independent of the individual. Organizations have storage systems, cognitive maps, memories, myths, ideologies (Hedberg, 1981) which, like the human brain, contain principles, guidelines, values, and hypotheses about internal and external relationships. Organizational storage systems record relationships, guidelines and processes, and keep them in the organization's 'memory' (Walsh and Ungson, 1991).

When information is stored in organizational 'knowledge systems', operational patterns are preserved. The behaviours and actions of individuals are transformed into lasting, replicable knowledge possessed by the organization. Organizational learning cannot be equated with individual learning processes and behaviours. For one thing, the knowledge of individuals has some components which are not known or accessible to the organization (Argyris and Schön, 1978: 9; Hedberg, 1981: 6). For another, organizations can store in their knowledge systems components which are no longer present in the knowledge stores of individuals (Argyris and Schön, 1978; Fiol and Lyles, 1985). Consequently, the organization may possess either more knowledge or less knowledge than all the individuals together.

It is easy to see how an organization may have less knowledge than the sum of its individual members. It is more difficult to see how it could have more; but this is in fact possible. It can happen, for example, if groups develop patterns of behaviour, based on shared experiences, which cannot be explained entirely in terms of the intentions and likely behaviours of individuals.

> **Organizational learning is unique to an institution. Organizational learning is both quantitatively and qualitatively distinct from the sum of the learning processes of individuals.**

The outcome of an organizational learning process is qualitatively different from the sum of individual learning processes. Institutions as a whole often behave differently from individuals: human interactions, the sharing of experiences, and discussions often trigger changes which affect the outcomes of learning. The following example illustrates the difference between individual and organizational learning.

The directors of a large company held a meeting to discuss the restructuring of a business unit. As input for the meeting, each member of top management had prepared a solution considering all functional areas. Everyone at the meeting had thus previously tackled the problem in his or her own way, working individually. The meeting was held in the presence of a neutral external observer. This observer checked the solutions of the participants for obvious inconsistencies, thus permitting an open and informative exchange of opinions. The distorting effect of 'political' statements was thus largely avoided.

At the meeting, expectations and standards were revealed, the norms of the company were considered, and the participants' ways of thinking and acting led to the development of a new kind of decision-making process. The team's final joint decision was completely different in kind from the individual suggestions. Through interaction, organizational learning had taken place.

Individual attempts may be made to solve a problem, and this may lead to individual learning processes. However, a decision made by a group can have implications for the organization which are entirely different from the implications of the sum of individual decisions. This is a result of interactions within the group and the sharing of experiences and frames of reference (Figure 7).

> **Organizational learning takes place through the medium of individuals and their interactions, which together constitute a different whole, with its own capabilities and characteristics. Learning by a social system cannot be equated with the sum of the learning processes undergone by individuals, and the outcomes of these processes. The individual processes and outcomes are nevertheless prerequisites for organizational learning and form an important basis for it.**

Organizational learning thus possesses an independent quality which distinguishes it from individual learning. This quality derives chiefly from the interactions between different members of the organization and in the relationship of the members to the whole. By analogy, the performance of a volleyball team cannot be equated with the sum of the abilities of the individual players or their style of play. Golfers, on the other hand, are autonomous players, because of the nature of the game.

We may now ask what it is that distinguishes learning by individuals from organizational learning. What is it that constitutes the move from the first level to the second, and how can it be brought about? A bridge must be built between the individual and the collective (Klimecki et al., 1994). We have already seen that learning by individuals may be defined as 'a change in behaviour or potential behaviour in a particular situation traceable to repeated experiences in that situation, and where the behavioural changes cannot be explained in terms of innate reactions, maturation, or passing states' (Bower and Hilgard, 1983: 31). Learning is thus a function of four factors:

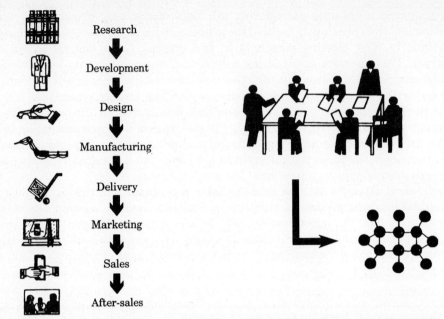

Research

Development

Design

Manufacturing

Delivery

Marketing

Sales

After-sales

Source: World Competitiveness Report, 1992

Figure 7 Decision-making by interdisciplinary groups.

- Cognitive structures, which influence the ways in which knowledge is taken in
- Intelligence
- Experience, in the sense of socially transmitted knowledge and acquired skills
- Previously developed situation-specific needs and motives

To this we may add interests and values relating to a particular object, and the level of difficulty of the material to be learned. This definition of individual learning is characterized by:

- Individual thinking
- Attachment to personal experience
- Links with individual needs and motives, interests and values
- The level of difficulty of the object of the task/material to be learned
- Manifestation in multiple behavioural changes

Organizational learning, on the other hand, is characterized by collective thinking and the creation of a shared frame of reference. The emphasis is not on individual motives, needs and values, but on experiential worlds which transcend the individual; on processes for making collectively binding decisions, and on an accepted order which brings about agreement in the form of majority decisions. This knowledge base, which serves as a foundation for making changes, is accessible to all and is driven by collectively agreed individual knowledge structures (Walsh, 1995). Organizational learning is not just a process of retrospective adaptation to problematic environmental situations, or of developing know-how for dealing with them; it is also a process of adaptation to needs, motives and interests within the organization, and to the values of its members.

It is clear that organizational learning differs from learning by individuals in that it involves a shared reality formed from the needs, motives and values of various members of the organization. An organizational or collectively constructed view of reality can only develop if individuals are prepared to discuss and negotiate their individual views. This makes the experiences of individuals accessible to all.

According to Fiol (1994), there is another factor which is necessary to the development of a collective view of reality, or shared frame of reference, and which is therefore necessary to learning. This factor is the performance of the apparently contradictory task of generating diversity while at the same time achieving consensus. It seems that members of the organization must agree and disagree at the same time. The goal is to unify the diversity by reaching a multidimensional consensus. Learning thus implies the development of new understanding. This results from the process of changing cognitive maps or social constructions of reality. The acquisition and interpretation of fresh knowledge brings about changes in cognitive maps; this in turn affects the range of potential behaviours. The ability to acquire and share common knowledge demands both divergence and convergence of the meanings that members of the organization attach to it. These meanings result from the pattern of communication, and therefore from the manner of expression. According to Cohen and Levinthal (1990), the challenge is to find a balance between diversity and consensus.

Several conditions must be met before the step from individual learning to organizational learning can be taken (Figure 8). According to Klimecki *et al.* (1994), the move depends on:

■ communication
■ transparency
■ integration

The development of a collective view of reality depends on mutual understanding by means of language, i.e. on *communication*. Without communication, there can be no agreement about reality or on the action which reality suggests. The knowledge of individuals cannot be made available to the organization, and there can be no collective discussion leading to a shared frame of reference.

Communication is not, however, sufficient in itself. If individual knowledge is to be transformed into organizational knowledge, the processes and outcomes of communication must be made accessible and transparent to all members of

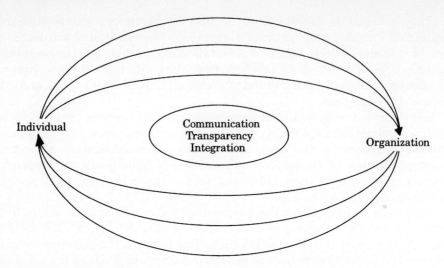

Figure 8 Transformational conditions for organizational learning.

the organization. *Transparency* presupposes the existence of a medium in which knowledge and symbolic values can be stored. Organizations therefore fix their main ideas in the form of management principles, vision and mission statements, histories or other symbolic forms. These forms of storage have an instrumental value, since they permit access to the organization. If individual learning processes are to be made part of the organization, they must be made transparent to all, so that people can reflect on them.

The third requirement for bridging the gap between individual learning and organizational learning is the *integration* of group processes into the system. If the knowledge of individuals is to be made available to the organization, then those individuals must be able to integrate their actions into the whole. Individuals need an integrated structure to support their own personal development; the organization needs it to facilitate organizational action. Figure 9 shows the transformational bridge between individual learning and organizational learning.

3   Theories of action

Argyris and Schön (1978) use the term 'theories of action' to refer to the organization's store of knowledge. The concept of theories of action, which they use both at individual and at organizational level, enables them to give a closer description of the store of knowledge and values; they use it to mean

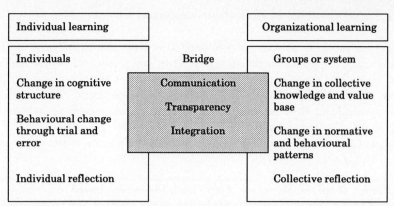

Figure 9 Transformational bridge between individual and organizational learning.

'expectations about the consequences of particular behaviours under specific conditions' (Pawlowsky, 1992). Theories of action, based on vision and mission statements, strategies, goals, culture, structures and power relations, constitute the frame of reference of the organization. This frame of reference determines the picture which the public and employees have of the company. The theories are the formal or informal expression of the economic, political, social and ecological goals of the organization.

The term 'theories of action' is used because these are theories upon which organizations or individuals base their activities. First, the theory of action must find a broad consensus within the organization to provide the company with an identity. This consensus is based on policies favoured by top management and on the views of smaller groups within the company that are in a position to observe changes in the environment and to determine a course accordingly. Charismatic leaders can play an important part in setting clear goals and guidelines because they provide a vision and a mission. They exert a dynamic influence and may set learning processes in motion. When members of the organization examine and analyze information and values, a picture of the company emerges; this can serve as a basis for further action. The processes of analysis give rise to a *frame of reference* within which individuals can develop. This frame of reference makes the actions of the system intelligible. It also enables individuals to learn in the work setting, so that in new situations they can act in ways which are compatible with the whole.

> **Theories of action form a frame of reference for the organization with respect to its continuity and the qualities essential for its continued existence.**

Following Argyris and Schön (1978), we distinguish two kinds of theories of action: official theories and 'theories in use'.

3.1 Official theories of action, or espoused theories

Official theories of action, or espoused theories, are the formal or informal expression of the goals of the company. They are ideas and values according to which individuals or organizations officially direct their actions (Argyris and Schön, 1978). There is usually broad agreement on them within the organization, and they normally spring from management principles held by the leaders. To understand the patterns of action generated by the system, employees must learn to recognize the frame of reference of the organization.

[handwritten margin note: link to slank works]

> Official theories of action (espoused theories), based on vision and mission statement, purpose, strategies, goals, culture and structure, form the framework of the organization. This framework is officially shared by the members of the organization; it determines their image of the company — the image to which they commit themselves.

If a company as a whole is to possess its own corporate identity, there must be broad agreement on basics amongst its members; this provides the frame of reference or image of the whole organization. Charismatic leaders cannot by themselves create an identity: there must also be a consensus across the company on this image. Companies often express their frames of reference in vision and mission statements covering the whole organization. Through these vision and mission statements, members of the organization acknowledge a degree of commitment to certain attitudes and behavioural principles.

3.2   Theories in use

Theories in use are defined by Argyris and Schön as theories from which real courses of action can be derived, or which unite in themselves the values embodied in the life of the organization. Individuals are not usually conscious of them, and they are not publicly discussed. They arise from interactions between individuals.

The organization's store of experience and knowledge determines how the organization behaves as an institution. Since every human society needs a rationale for its actions, knowledge is objectivized by individual members of organizations, and this leads to a basic consensus on coexistence (Berger and Luckmann, 1990). This basic consensus — or the 'intersubjective view of reality' — provides the members of the organization with hypotheses about organizational behaviour. These hypotheses form the basis for a process of agreement which makes knowledge within the organization usable and communicable.

> **An organization's theories in use are the outcome of individual and group experiences and the interactions between them, and of comparisons of experiences against the institutional framework.**

If the actions of an organization produce unexpected results, expectations are questioned and may be adjusted. Discrepancies between espoused theories and theories in use trigger organizational learning processes.

4 How we recognize organizational learning

When discrepancies between espoused theories and theories in use are noticed and discussed, organizational learning processes are set in motion. We now consider how we may describe and recognize these processes.

In the course of their development, individuals evolve cognitive patterns which influence their perception and interpretation of situations. These cognitive patterns are responsible for individual and collective views of reality. Just as individuals possess cognitive patterns, so organizations develop knowledge structures in the course of interactive processes. Organizational researchers have described these knowledge structures in different ways, e.g. as organizational doctrines (Nystrom and Starbuck, 1984); organizational frames of reference (Shrivastava, 1983); mental or cognitive maps of the organization (Weick and Bougon, 1986); organizational knowledge base (Pautzke, 1989); intersubjective views of reality (Berger and Luckmann, 1990); and knowledge structures (Walsh, 1995).

Central to the concept of knowledge structures is the organizational aspect, i.e. the sharing of knowledge by interacting individuals. Sackmann (1991, 1992) distinguishes four kinds of shared knowledge:[1]

- **Dictionary knowledge**: This is descriptive knowledge (the 'what'). It contains the descriptions which are shared by members of the organization, i.e. the definitions and references that are used throughout the system. It embraces language customs and terminology, e.g. customer satisfaction, customer focus, efficiency, lean management.
- **Directory knowledge**: This is procedural knowledge (the 'how'). It embraces generally shared practices, and includes knowledge about cause-and-effect relationships and chains of events. It answers questions like, 'What leads to customer satisfaction?', or 'What influences the market?'

---

[1] We believe that Sackmann's (1992) division of knowledge into the categories described above may also be used as a classification of cognitive structures.

- **Recipe knowledge**: This is prescriptive knowledge (the 'should'). It offers instructions and recommendations, based on certain shared norms. This kind of knowledge includes guidelines for action such as quality levels (ISO 9000), production times, choice of suppliers and benchmarking.
- **Axiomatic knowledge**: This is knowledge about reasons and causes (the 'why'). It contains the premises for organizational action. Examples are goal-setting, formulations of company policies and basic values underlying business activity.

These kinds of knowledge form the framework for learning and action. The four kinds of knowledge form integral parts of cognitive patterns. Most authors refer to them as schemata, mental plans or cognitive maps. These cognitive patterns or intersubjective views of reality develop as a result of the transfer of information from one member of an organization to another, or from one group to another (Simon, 1991). The relationships between the knowledge of the members and the organizational memory may be considered responsible for the collective process of creating meaning.

Organizational learning is triggered when a discrepancy becomes apparent between currently professed principles (espoused theories) and actual action (theories in use). The learning process consists in making changes to the kinds of knowledge described by Sackmann (1992). The changes lead to an increase in the range of possible behaviours.

The process of organizational learning is characterized by:

- **Change in organizational knowledge**
- **Increase in the range of possible actions**
- **Change in intersubjective constructions of reality**

The range of possible behaviours forms the basis for the development of strategies for action. The goal of organizational learning must therefore be to increase the range of possible behaviours by making changes in collective knowledge.

Although organizational learning is intuitively easily recognized, a wide range of possible conceptions of learning exist in the literature. This chapter aims to integrate the different conceptions. There remain, however, distinct approaches towards learning. In the overview shown in Figure 10, the conceptions of different authors have been summarized to provide the reader with a comprehensive picture of possible conceptions of learning. This summary shows the various definitions as well as the subject, content and method of learning.

Authors	Definition	Who? (subject of learning)	What? (content of learning)	How? (learning processes)
Cyert and March (1963)	Organizational learning is adaptive behavior of organizations over time	Organizational level	Standard operating procedures and organizational rules	Adaptation of goals and rules, learning by experience
Argyris and Schön (1978)	Organizational learning is the process in which organizational members detect errors or anomalies and correct them by restructuring the organizational theory in use	Individuals in organizations	Organizational theories in use and theories of action	Assumption sharing, individual and collective inquiry, modification of theories in use
Duncan and Weiss (1979)	Organizational learning is the process within the organization by which knowledge about action/outcome relationships and the effect on the environment on these relationships is developed	Individuals and their interaction	Organizational knowledge base	Development of action/outcome relationships through sharing, evaluation or integration
Hedberg (1981)	Organizational learning is the process through which members acquire and process information through interaction with their environment in order to increase their understanding of reality by observing the results of their action	Individuals learn in organizations. Organizations are the stage of action	Cognitive systems, myths, theories of action	Experimental learning, learning by imitation
Fiol and Lyles (1985)	Organizational learning is the process of improving actions through better knowledge and understanding	Organizational learning is more than the sum of individual learning	Patterns of cognitive associations and/or new responses of action	Development of complex associations
Levitt and March (1988)	Organizations are seen as learning by encoding inferences from history into routine behaviour	Organizational learning has an emergent component	Routines, e.g. rules, procedures, framework, culture, belief structures, etc.	Learning from direct experience or experience of others, learning of paradigms for interpretation
Huber (1991)	Organizational learning means processing information to increase the range of potential behaviours	Entities learn. Entities are individuals, groups, organizations, industries, etc.	Information and knowledge	Information processing, acquisition, distribution, interpretation, storage
Weick and Roberts (1993)	Organizational learning consists of interrelating actions of individuals	Connections between behaviours rather than individuals	Behaviour or action	Interrelationship between contribution, representation and subordination

Source: adapted from Prange, 1996.

Figure 10 Overview of learning conceptions.

Case study 2

Jakob Schläpfer Ltd

Jakob Schläpfer Ltd has a modern network structure and a culture which is creative and strongly oriented towards learning. How have these things come about? What are the difficulties in putting the underlying ideas into practice?

Schläpfer Ltd, which has nearly 140 employees, is one of the best-known Swiss exporters of embroidery. The firm is based in St. Gallen, Paris, Los Angeles and Osaka, and produces primarily for the fashion market. Almost all of its products go to leading fashion houses such as Armani and Lacroix. In the past thirty years, Jakob Schläpfer Ltd has been a leading influence in textile technology for the manufacture of embroidery and similar fashion products. The textile designers produce four collections per year, amounting to more than 1,400 designs, using embroidery, sequins and fashionable designer fabrics. The company's work and culture are therefore strongly oriented towards creativity. The products are manufactured on the firm's premises or on those of contract suppliers; each run is subjected to a detailed in-house quality check. The firm's philosophy contains the following credo:

> Our success as a company has always depended on our creativity: we do not copy what others are already doing; we work according to our own ideas. This is true in a literal sense of our collections, and indirectly true of all our other activities: we solve our problems creatively.

Over the years, management based on creativity has led to the emergence of a corresponding philosophy.

'Management' supported creative thinking and the human community; the management hierarchy is a flat pyramid. Many new organigrams were developed, but neither the employees nor the management were ever really satisfied with them. Finally, a solution was found in the form of so-called networks. The idea was the outcome of workshops held in the firm's own creative centre in Tessin, and of the ideas of Robert Schläpfer, who practises a paternal style of leadership. The network concept offered a definite and distinctive identity. It was expressed in the company philosophy 'which is based on congruence between the business goals and intrinsic goals of the employees and of the company, and which seeks to harmonize the necessary purpose of every business action with the spirit of human creativity' (Figure 11). Lisbet and Robert Schläpfer withdrew to a large extent from the management of the company, leaving the employees as non-voting shareholders. They were replaced by a tighter, younger leadership, which functions largely as a network group and has no permanent director. Committed employees of many years' experience form a wider circle of advisers and leaders, thus extending the network principle. Figure 12 shows how all employees are responsible for realizing the company's goals.

In the firm's own 'school', in the Creative Centre, employees have an opportunity to develop their creativity and to form a cohesive community. Officially espoused theories rarely appear in the company's documentation: the few examples include the statement of company philosophy, a few lectures and a general guidance document. A

The business goal of the company is to increase its value

This involves:

- Profit
- Capital
- Reserves
- Welfare funds
- Means of production
- Know-how and patents
- Organization

The intrinsic goal of the company is to act in accordance with its own identity

This involves:

- Freedom and independence of action
- Stability and continuity in performance
- Reliability
- Trustworthiness
- Openness and ability to innovate
- Inspiring respect and exerting influence
- Combining success with self-awareness and self-confidence

The basic goal of all employees is to improve their own prosperity

This involves:

- Income, savings and property
- Insurances
- Professional ability
- Freedom
- Pleasant place of work
- Society
- Enough money to make donations and gifts

The intrinsic goals of our employees are to have confidence in themselves, to take pleasure in their achievements at work, and to enjoy their lives

This involves:

- A feeling of belonging, of security, and of being protected
- Working with dedication as part of a community
- Working responsibly to complete their own tasks
- Educating and developing themselves
- Being able to respect themselves and others
- Combining success with self-awareness and self-confidence
- Being able to give of themselves

Source: Schläpfer company document, 1993

Figure 11 Business and intrinsic goals of Schläpfer.

Who is responsible for the attainment of goals?

Every member of the company.

Our success depends on everyone acting responsibly.
To enable all members to work responsibly and to attain
their common goals together and in harmony, all those in
leadership positions must lead responsibly.

This is our view of responsibility in action and in leadership.

Source: Schläpfer, 1993

Figure 12 Responsibility for goal attainment in Schläpfer.

deliberate attempt is made to avoid documentation, for fear of creating something artificial, and 'talking (or writing) the idea to death'. It is interesting to note, however, that rules governing behaviour and speech have grown up spontaneously in the company, and that these rules embody and support the network style of functioning. Terms such as 'executive', 'specialist', 'boss' are not used by the employees. Instead, they talk about network consultants and networkers. This means that each member of the network shares responsibility for the attainment of objectives.

The company tries to operate the network as a fluid system constantly seeking its own level. This system allows competent decisions to be made in many places at the same time, since everybody takes part in the process, assimilates it and passes it on. This means that, in practice, the change from 'supervisor' to 'network consultant' and 'subordinate' to 'networker' is more than just a play on words. For both 'network consultants' and 'networkers', views of responsibility are bound up with individual views of freedom. 'The right of a network consultant is the right to give more, not the right to be omniscient and omnipotent, and to have to fix everything to the point of

personal exhaustion. This kind of giving is a real pleasure; learning how to do it can be an electrifying experience.'

In Jakob Schläpfer Ltd, visions arise within the working community which produces the results. The community in turn constantly remoulds itself according to new values. The process is one of self-determination. The company does not live by endless and unsatisfactory theories and ideals. Instead, it determines the critical success factors, and then deduces from them what cannot be allowed to go wrong. Everything else follows. This transmission of negative feedback through the network has proved successful.

■ Our company is a dynamic network of interdependent elements which influence each other.
■ The activity of the company is shaped by the combined influence of three factors: the network consultants, the employees and the situation.
■ The network consultant is a person who has unique strengths, but who also has weaknesses and goal conflicts.
■ Employees are to be given a

> **large degree of independence in carrying out and checking their work.**
> ■ **This means that the most important element in every inspection system is responsible self-inspection.**

Nevertheless, we find frequent discrepancies between the espoused theories and the theories in use. Network thinking clearly works for the employees who are involved in creative work or who deal with customers, assemble the collection, etc. However, members of the management often find themselves in the position of network consultees in situations where they no longer make the decisions, and they keep quiet to avoid discomfort. Networking becomes painful and leads to doubts and unease when a discrepancy is discovered between espoused theories and theories in use. It is even more difficult when an employee is relieved that the 'boss' has taken over a decision, 'because he is the "boss", and ought to know best'.

Gaps such as these became especially noticeable during the difficult times of the recession, and they were much discussed during that period (1992/93). When meetings are held to discuss particular topics, everyone expresses an opinion and there is an atmosphere of openness. However, no decisions are taken. Problems are often aggravated by a failure to make decisions, and time then becomes the most important factor. Decisions can become superfluous for various reasons, for

example 'the system' decides instead of the people, or authority intervenes and takes the decision away from the group, or projects die.

Discrepancies between espoused theories and theories in use are not, however, without value. They can precipitate the process of organizational learning.

With the aim of promoting organizational learning, workshops were held in the Creative Centre to analyze theories of leadership and ways of working together and making decisions. Anomalies were identified and discussed, for example in connection with unavoidable redundancies, new sales concepts, financial decisions on projects. These discussions led to an increase in shared knowledge, since the interactive exchange of information increased the range of possible behaviours. The discussions resulted in a changed frame of reference, and a foundation was laid for further action. In this way, the strategies for action and problem-solving were multiplied.

The significance of fluctuating, intermittent hierarchies (heterarchies) was analyzed and discussed, decision-making processes were developed, and responsibilities and expectations were defined (Hedlund, 1986). The learning process was particularly fruitful in relation to acceptance of temporary leadership structures, exercise of power, exposure of conflicts, and the drawing of a wide circle of employees into advisory functions. The opportunity for organizational learning was thus exploited.

WORKSHEET II		
Analysis of the organization's store of knowledge		
	Which of the following kinds of knowledge are especially well-developed? Comments:	What form do they take?
Dictionary knowledge: Jargon, terminology, etc. *Examples*: customer satisfaction; quality; lean management		
Directory knowledge: How does event X affect event Y? *Example*: quality improvement leads to customer satisfaction		
Recipe knowledge: Instructions for action, guidance, rules *Examples*: steps in problem-solving; customer consultation every two months		
Axiomatic knowledge: Values, policies, attitudes *Examples*: 'All customers must be treated in a friendly manner'; 'If we can buy environmentally friendly products of the same quality at no great extra cost, we will do so'		

WORKSHEET II (continued)

Does my company have official values which it often fails to put into practice?

Give examples to show the difference between your company's official theories of action (espoused theories) as they appear in vision and mission statements, organizational rules, instructions, etc. and the theories in use which are actually applied (e.g. team skills, motivational measures, problem-solving strategies, ability to deal with conflict, etc.).

	Official theory of action	Theory in use
Group		
Division/business unit		
Company		

3

What is the nature of organizational learning?

Learning involves change in organizational knowledge in the broadest sense. The process of change can affect several kinds of knowledge at the same time, and the depth and content of the change can vary. Learning processes can therefore be classified into different categories. We distinguish among three different levels of learning:

- Adaptive learning
- Reconstructive learning
- Process learning

1 Adaptive learning

When members of an organization interact with the internal and external environments, their perceptions of reality change continually, as new information is gained and old information is lost. During this process, stimulus/response chains are broken and may be re-formed (Hedberg, 1981). The amount of new information may be relatively small, and the changes therefore slight; the need for change may be seen as arising from mistakes in theories in use (Argyris and Schön, 1978), and these mistakes may be corrected. When this happens, the company has learned to adapt, by changing its behaviour. Cyert and March (1963) describe this process in terms of adjustments in search rules and attention rules, and changes of indicators. This emphasizes the behavioural and instrumental character of the change.

For the first level of learning, we have used the term *adaptive learning*,

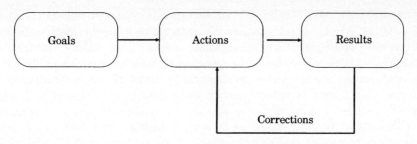

Source: based on Argyris and Schön, 1978

Figure 13 Adaptive, or single-loop, learning.

because the organization adapts to its environment (see Case study 3 on the training department in ABB). Members of the organization are able to identify problems in their environment, develop strategies for dealing with them, and implement those strategies. Adaptive learning therefore consists simply in adapting behaviour towards the attainment of the existing goals. Continuing to use Argyris and Schön's terminology, we may say that this learning process is the reaction of the organization to its internal and external environments: the organization reacts by correcting errors in the theories in use to bring them back into line with existing norms. Argyris and Schön describe this process as 'single-loop learning', since the system is regulated according to an existing norm (Figure 13).

The stimulus for this kind of learning is the gap between objectives and outcomes. Deviations from given norms are corrected by a process of adaptation so as to redirect behaviour towards existing goals. The old theories of action are changed (Argyris and Schön, 1978). We could also express this by saying that the organization has adapted to difficulties presented by the environment, and that this process has taken place within the framework of the existing values and interests of individual group members or subcultures. The learning process is determined by norms and values which form part of the organization's own rationale. This means that the organization adjusts to environmental factors, but existing norms and values are not questioned: they remain directed towards the existing purpose of the company.

> **Adaptive learning is the process of adjusting effectively to given goals and norms by mastering the environment.**

2 Reconstructive learning

The next level of learning involves not only behavioural adaptation but also changes in deeper, cognitive structures. Significant changes occur in the relationship between the organization and its environment, necessitating more than a simple process of adaptation. *Reconstructive learning* involves facing up to internal conflicts. Organizational norms and values which seem unchangeable must nevertheless be questioned; new priorities must be set, and new evaluations made. Value systems may have to be restructured. The organization's frame of reference can only continue to develop if existing knowledge structures are changed and the behavioural repertoire is modified (see Case study 4). New theories of action emerge; this leads to a critical examination of values and norms, which in turn changes the image and the underlying structure of the organization.

Whatever the nature of the organizational learning process, its results can only be described as learning outcomes if they are recognized and accepted as useful by the members of the system. The concept of organizational learning focuses on the needs, motives, interests and values embedded within the structure of the organization. This means that cognitive processes may be regarded as having functional content (i.e. as being useful and accepted) if they lead to learning processes which involve the needs, motives, interests and values of the community, whether past, present or future. It follows from this that reconstructive learning does not simply mean adapting to environmental problems or developing the know-how to deal with them. It implies changes in the interests and values of individual group members or of subgroups whose behaviour may be antagonistic to the attainment of a goal or the accomplishment of a task. Learning is usually a rationally based process, but reason can conflict with the aims of the organization (e.g. it may be reasonable to ban advertising by the cigarette industry, but this is not necessarily reasonable from the point of view of the industry).

Questioning the organization's frame of reference means confronting its hypotheses, and this may lead to modification of its goals. Argyris and Schön (1978) describe this process as 'double-loop learning' since it involves a critical examination of theories of action; this leads to questioning of the original goals, which are then changed (Figure 14).

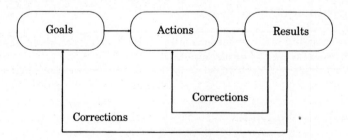

Source: based on Argyris and Schön, 1978

Figure 14 Reconstructive, or double-loop, learning.

Argyris and Schön (1978) regard *open provision of information* as the most important condition for reconstructive learning. Hedberg (1981) considers the *unlearning* of learning cycles to be vital. Neither of these points is easy to achieve. Kelly (1955) says that the pictures or 'cognitive maps' which members form of an organization tend towards rigidity, because people's socially constructed views of reality and the logical interconnections between them confirm existing perceptions and norms. Signals are then ignored for as long as possible, until there is sufficient counter-evidence to justify radical organizational change.

Reconstructive learning is the process of questioning organizational norms and values, and building a new frame of reference.

---

3 Process learning

Most authors agree that the process of changing cognitive maps, or of 'reframing', is a difficult one (Hedberg, 1981; Watzlawick, 1988; Argyris, 1990). In most cases, defensive routines have been built up. Individuals, groups and organizations are unlikely to become aware either of their routines or of their errors, and they are thus protected from the threat of change (Argyris, 1990). Experience teaches us that change is associated with uncertainty and ambiguity. 'Fundamental rules' therefore develop; these ensure that errors are ignored, or not discussed, and that their non-discussability is also not discussed. (For further treatment of the difficulties of unlearning, see Chapter 6.) At this higher level of learning, changes in the frame of reference are of great importance. The success of the learning process and the restructuring of values and norms may be judged according to usefulness and the degree of acceptance of change within the organization. If several members of the organization agree on new values, or if such agreement is reached between groups, learning processes of a higher order have taken place.

The organization as a whole and its individual members often understand the significance and necessity of learning as just described, but defensive routines prevent it from happening. Intervention at this level of learning is fruitless, for the reasons given above. The first step must therefore be to explain the nature of learning processes. The processes of adaptive learning and reconstructive learning, and the difficulties associated with them, must be explained to members of the organization if successful reconstructive learning is to take place. This process of *learning to learn* is the highest level of learning. The aim is not to learn particular items of information, but rather to study the process of learning itself.

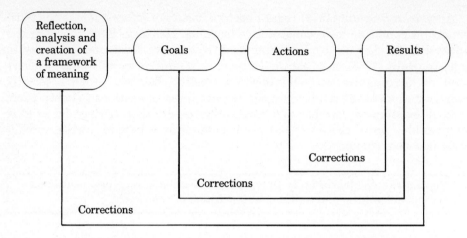

Source: based on Argyris and Schön, 1978

Figure 15 Process learning.

Our picture of the different levels of learning is now complete. According to Bateson (1981), learning at the highest level — *process learning* — embraces all phenomena which fall under the heading of changes in the stream of action and experience, together with changes in the use of context markers. In other words, process learning is learning to understand adaptive and reconstructive learning. The central element in process learning is the improvement of the ability to learn; the subject of learning is learning itself. The recognition of patterns which have enabled learning to take place in similar situations can lead to a comprehensive restructuring of behavioural rules and norms.

As shown in Figure 15, process learning involves reflection, analysis and the creation of a framework of meaning. This implies gaining insight into the learning process itself, into the solving of the problems in context, and into the unfolding of learning processes. It is only when this level is reached that the individual can study his own role and see himself as the environment of other social systems (Willke, 1991).

Reflection is a form of participation, since it takes into account the conditions necessary for others in the environment to survive and develop. If members of the organization are able to reflect, and to learn how to learn, possible conflicts can be anticipated, their likely consequences evaluated, and opportunities assessed for making internal corrections. The individual can optimize his or her own environment, and at the same time derive maximum benefit from a structure of relationships involving several participants.

> **Process learning consists of gaining insight into the learning process. It means learning to learn.**

When a system learns to learn, its internal relationships are seen more clearly, and this can lead to transformation of the organization. The pattern of interrelationships within the system, and between the system and its environment, become recognizable. These insights into the patterns of relationships and the likely consequences of action can lead to changes in the underlying structure of the organization. The emphasis is on achieving awareness, on reflecting and on recognizing patterns. The learning process is directed not towards procedures, principles or goals in themselves, but towards understanding the meaning of the organization.

Different authors have referred to the different levels of learning in a number of ways. Figure 16 provides an analysis of the range of terms used to describe those different levels.

	Learning type 1 Adaptive learning	Learning type 2 Reconstructive learning	Learning type 3 Process learning
Pawlowsky (1992)	Idiosyncratic adaptation	Adaptation to environment	Learning to solve problems
Argyris and Schön (1978)	Single-loop learning	Double-loop learning	Deutero-learning
Klimecki et al. (1991)	Improvement learning	Change learning	Learning to learn
Sattelberger (1991c)	Organizational change	Organizational development	Organizational transformation
Senge (1990)	Adaptive learning		Generative learning
Garratt (1990)	Operational learning circle	Policy learning circle	Integrated learning circle
Morgan (1986)	Single-loop	Double-loop	Holographic learning
Pautzke (1989)	Raising efficiency	Learning from experience	Change in knowledge structures
Staehle (1991)	Assimilation	Accommodation	Equilibration
Hedberg (1981)	Adjustment learning	Turnover learning	Turnaround learning
Shrivastava (1983)	Adaptation	Assumption sharing	Development of knowledge base
Fiol and Lyles (1985)	Lower-level learning	Higher-level learning	
Bateson (1981)	Type I learning		Deutero-learning
Duncan and Weiss (1979)	Adaptation		
March and Olsen (1976)	Adaptation		
Cyert and March (1963)	Adaptation		
Cangelosi and Dill (1965)	Adaptation		

Figure 16 Classification of organizational learning terminology.

Case study 3 ———————————————————————————

Organizational learning at departmental level: the training department in ABB

ABB is a young company which was created by the merger of two industrial firms: ASEA of Sweden and Brown Boveri of Switzerland. The merger was seen as a step into the future. The firm's motto is 'Think global, act local'; this reveals its intention to combine market orientation with customer orientation. ABB Switzerland in Baden has 14,000 employees and thirty-five autonomous company units, making it one of ABB's largest subsidiaries.

In response to internal and external changes, the entire human resource department of ABB Switzerland undertook an analysis of the firm's strategy. The department developed a new strategy for the whole company; this strategy, which sets the standard for future measures, is to be implemented by all employees engaged in human resource activities. The standard is distributed to the decentralized departments in the form of a set of principles and goals (Figure 17).[1] In accordance with ABB internal policy, it is then up to each human resource department to achieve these goals.

When members of the ABB training department try to analyze their internal training programme in order to fulfil the aims of the human resource strategy, and the training programme changes as a result of this analysis, adaptive learning will have taken place. If the department changes its internal actions and programmes in order to

achieve a given goal, it will have adapted to that goal, in this case the human resource strategy. The members of the department will act according to the goals that have been agreed. In adapting to the goals set out in the ABB human resource policy document, the training department will have learned and will have changed its training programme.

However, if the same department analyzes the hypotheses and assumptions basic to its environment, and its own attitude towards the ABB human resource policy, and produces a new (training) programme (which differs from the human resource strategy), then it will have carried out a thorough analysis of the values of the organization. This analysis could lead to changed values for teamwork. The training department will have noted the goals which have been set but will not have accepted them without reservation. It will have taken them as guidelines for its own analysis, and shaped the content in its own way. The changes to the training programme will thus be the result of an analysis of the goals of ABB, of internal goals, and of the values which lie behind them.

In the first of these situations, the members of the training department come to terms with the goals which have been set for internal training. This means that they keep their goals in sight and try to develop strategies which will enable them to reach them. The learning process consists in adapting themselves to the environment, and may therefore be called *adaptive learning*.

In the second situation, organizational

---

[1] The ABB human resource policy covers the following areas among others: coping with change; education and further training; management development; furthering women's careers.

Aims of human resource policy

We aim to achieve the greatest possible harmony between the *interests of our employees* on the one hand and the overall *interests of the company* on the other. The closer we come to realizing this aim, the better we can fulfil our responsibilities towards our clients, our investors, the environment and the area within which we operate.

Education and training

ABB Switzerland has a great interest in an educational system which is of high quality, and which is adjusted to the needs of the economy and society. We therefore encourage all our employees to offer their experience and skills in management committees of educational institutions. We are also active in influencing the Swiss educational system.

Our employees face ever-changing demands; our success depends in large measure on our ability to learn. We must therefore remain constantly aware of the *core demands* placed upon our employees, and the *skills* which are needed to meet them. Where there is a gap between demands and skills, there is a need for further training; we fulfil further training requirements in order of priority and as effectively as possible. The emphasis is on further training in the immediate working context.

In addition to development of specialized skills, we attach great importance to the development of *personality* and *social competence*. The improvement of *leadership qualities* (ability to lead both people and organizations) is a permanent requirement for managers at all levels.

ABB Switzerland has an *education support group* which provides the ABB communities with systems and methods for determining further training needs. This group advises on how further training needs can best be met via the training market. The group guarantees to provide the organization with *further training in specialist skills specific to ABB*. For further training specific to ABB in the areas of personality, social competence and leadership (of people and companies), the group offers high-quality courses at market prices.

Each supervisor is *responsible* for the competence of his/her group members, though the members themselves are responsible for the quality of their work. We expect all employees to show initiative and application with regard to their own further training, both at their place of work and outside the company. Supervisors support their group members in their efforts to acquire further training, and advise them. The nature and extent of ABB involvement in the further training of their employees is the subject of individual agreements.

Source: ABB, 1992

Figure 17 Extract from ABB human resource policy, 1992.

norms and values are questioned and new priorities are set for future goals. As a result of this process, the current goals of the organization are not necessarily retained, but may be changed. This can lead to questioning and possible readjustment of the human resource policy which had already been decided for the whole of ABB. This kind of learning may be called *reconstructive learning* since it involves changing the existing frame of reference. The training department will have learned to analyze and to question existing values and norms.

Case study 4 ⸻

Organizational learning at institutional level: the restructuring of Digital Equipment (Europe)

Digital Equipment Corporation (DEC) is a world leader in the production of networked computer systems, software and services. In the early years of information technology, DEC was influential in shaping the industry, and was a pioneer in interactive multivendor computer networks. DEC is an international company which conducts a large part of its business outside the USA, primarily in Europe and Asia. It offers a broad range of products for a wide variety of customers, for example telecommunications companies, banks, industry.

In 1991/92, DEC decided to restructure in order to adapt to the requirements of major customers, and to develop a functional and nationally oriented matrix structure. The aim was to move towards more flexible and autonomous units which would nevertheless be joined into a network. The company planned to create 'a network of entrepreneurs in a global enterprise'; the object of the change was to achieve 'customer orientation'. This structure was to operate in different countries by building up a service or infrastructure function to provide know-how. Customer orientation through flexible network structures was to be implemented by spreading the so-called entrepreneurs in different business areas across different countries. For the whole of Europe, this meant that responsibility for the performance of twenty countries was transferred to three hundred entrepreneurs. The entrepreneurs, with their new responsibilities, were clearly intended to be the agents of change (Figure 18).

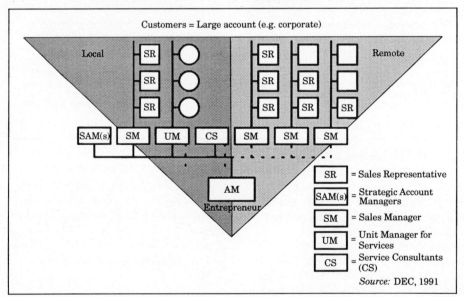

Figure 18 Organization based on entrepreneurs.

The diagram differentiates between the 'corporate' members of the organization who work in the head office, dealing with strategic aspects of customer service, and with sales and customer service as a whole (local); and members who work directly with customers (remote). Each major client has a structure of this kind at his disposal, with the entrepreneurs taking responsibility.

The new position of entrepreneurs enabled them to work within the basic organizational structure (infrastructure and services) to create rational solutions for the whole system, and to follow previously unexplored avenues. The organization was obliged to change, to question its values and norms, and to transform its existing structures. By questioning the existing structure, it learned to appraise its frame of reference. *Reconstructive learning* had taken place.

This, however, was not the only step in the learning process. The main emphasis was on the ability of the 'entrepreneurial units' to develop a quality of self-awareness which would permit them to organize themselves. The aim was to facilitate learning, in the context of new ways of operating and interacting, and the interdependencies which this created (Escher, 1993: 7). The entrepreneurs were in a position to make decisions in consultation with others, the only criterion being a rational structuring of activities. They had to bear in mind customer satisfaction and the general purpose of the organization; previously existing structures did not necessarily have to be used. Their attention was explicitly drawn to the fact that they were not expected to aim at structural standardization; on the contrary,

differences based on consensus would be welcomed. The opportunity for change enabled DEC to learn and to change its structure on the basis of new values and knowledge. The company set up a unique learning process. 'Instead of issuing a "decree", the company provided "tools" and "building blocks" for learning at several leadership fora held for future entrepreneurial candidates' (Escher, 1993). The only fixed elements were the basic organizational units and links in the form of operational principles and standards (e.g. standard reporting system, cost-recovery contributions for services, service-level agreements). Each entrepreneur could choose his own building blocks and combine them as he wished, depending on the demands made by his customers. The leadership fora gave the entrepreneurs an opportunity to think about a suitable structure for the future, and how to achieve it. They were given the tools for making changes. The process of reflection brought about learning at the highest level, namely *process learning*. The necessary conditions for this were the infrastructure which supported communication and information, and the interchange of ideas on the tools for learning. These elements provided the technological and behavioural basis for reaching a consensus, and thinking about possible ways ahead.

Today, DEC is again undergoing a process of reorganization and restructuring, this time in favour of nine customer- and product-oriented business units. However, this is not because of the success or failure of the learning process; it has more to do with the evolutionary dynamics of social systems (Escher, 1993).

WORKSHEET III

Analysis of forms of learning

■ Which forms of learning (adaptive, reconstructive, process) can you see in your company?

A. Describe instances of the following which you see in your working environment:

Adaptive learning	
Reconstructive learning	
Process learning	

Helpful questions

■ Have actions been carried out which improved goal attainment? (adaptive learning)
■ Have there been changes in values and norms? (reconstructive learning)
■ Have learning processes been evaluated? (process learning)

WORKSHEET III (continued)

B. Discuss your examples in your group, considering the following points:

Questions	Results of discussions
To what extent are these real learning processes?	
Are the situations which prompted learning consistent with the level of learning? (need for adaptive learning, reconstructive learning, process learning)	
Who was the main agent of the learning process?	

4

What triggers learning in organizations?

In the earlier chapters we introduced and defined the concept of organizational learning and discussed the levels at which it takes place. The next question is, why does learning actually happen, i.e. what triggers and drives learning processes?

Organizations cannot and should not be forever occupied with looking for ways to change. If they did, their continuity, identity and security would be threatened. Organizations therefore depend on standard procedures, according to which in situation X, they can react with plan Y. As a rule, whether change is needed depends on the existing structure of the company, on the knowledge to hand and on the needs for tomorrow. Where existing knowledge is preserved and standard procedures are not questioned, learning is hampered. So how can learning happen in spite of this? Stability and 'slack' resources can enable learning to take place; unfortunately, however, changes are much more often the result of conflicts, difficulties and crises.

It is helpful to start by distinguishing between two fundamentally different causes of learning:

■ Turbulence and crises
■ 'Slack' resources

1 Learning through turbulence and crises

Most learning processes are probably triggered by unsolved problems of various kinds. Learning can result from internal or external disturbances such as conflicts, dissatisfaction, weakening of structures, or competitive pressure. Amongst internal factors, employee dissatisfaction with unsolved issues seems to be the most frequent reason for seeking strategies for solving problems (March and Simon, 1958). Members of the organization begin to look for solutions when there is a gap between expectations and outcomes, or when the gap becomes obvious (March and Simon, 1958; Hedberg, 1981). Doubts about strategies lead to the examination and re-evaluation of current courses of action, and new solutions may be sought. Interpersonal conflicts arising from the discovery of gaps between outcomes and expectations can also lead to re-evaluation of interactions, and hence to learning. Decision makers tend to use an index which is a function of the relation between outcomes and expectations in order both to evaluate strategies and to bring about change if necessary (Hedberg, 1981).

Problems which lead company results to deviate from decision-makers' expectations can also trigger learning. This means that deviations and conflicts are not wholly negative: they can be put to good use. As an example, a disagreement between two leaders about plans to implement an employee participation programme could become the basis of a learning process.

Stress is another reason why organizations may look for solutions to problems; its presence may indicate a need for change or adaptation. Stress causes the system or subsystem to learn, under pressure from the environment or from the need to succeed. There are two possible sources of stress. Environmental or discomfort stress arises when the complexity and dynamics of the environment exceed the perceptual capacities of the members of the organization. Alternatively, stress can result from the need to succeed when the pressure to achieve certain goals is too high. Both these kinds of stress lead to changes in the behaviour of groups or individuals when the level of stress is so high that the conflict has to be resolved. Each organization has a different level of stress tolerance in relation to particular activities. This level depends on the norms of the organization, those of its environment and those of individuals. When groups experience stress which exceeds a certain level, i.e. when they can no longer cope with the divergences and conflicts, and are forced to confront the problem, then the whole system may learn. If problems at all levels of the organization become acute, leading to excessive stress, or if there is a wide gap between expectations and outcomes, management crises occur and reveal the need for learning processes.

In these ways, stress and the conflicts which arise can act as triggers for organizational learning and make institutions, groups and individuals aware of the need to act. If learning processes are actually to take place, the need for action must be recognized in time; otherwise, the dynamics and complexity of the environment and the pressure of the resultant problems can reach such proportions that it is too late to do anything. (In extreme cases, 'matters take their own course'.)

2 Learning as a result of slack

If the situations described above were the only triggers for learning, then organizations would not be capable of learning unless they had problems. However, Cyert and March (1963) have shown that companies need not be experiencing difficulties in order to learn. They can also learn when they have excess capacity, too many opportunities and an accumulation of resources. This is because successful organizations have the time and the resources to search their environment for new and innovative solutions, or to undertake timely analyses of existing solutions.

'Organizational slack', structural redundancy and loose coupling between organizational units are necessary conditions for flexibility, innovation and change, and for organizational learning. Organizational slack is defined as the difference between necessary and available resources; it refers to capacity for action which is not used up in the daily business and can therefore be used freely and creatively for learning processes. Redundancy, excess resources and loose coupling of partly autonomous organizational units permits the organization to act and react in time in situations characterized by uncertainty and complex and variable circumstances. Occasionally, the situation can be brought under control. Usually, managers complain about wasted time, duplication of effort, empty runs and surplus personnel. However, repetition and duplication constitute the slack which permits errors or faults in the system to be identified and corrected as quickly as possible. The immediate economic profit of a lean organization cannot be set against the loss of flexibility, creativity and ability to perceive opportunities, all of which are difficult to quantify, nor does it compensate for reduced ability to forestall crises (Staehle, 1991).

It is largely unclear how organizational slack actually triggers learning. On the one hand, the process of reducing slack can lead to learning. Slack can be reduced by restructuring, re-engineering or making other organizational changes (Hammer and Champy, 1993). On the other hand, surplus resources themselves can trigger learning. Where slack is present, innovative solutions can be developed and structural changes made, and these entail internal processes of learning and change. If good use is to be made of free capacity, redundancy must also be present. This may take the form of *redundancy within structures* or *redundancy of whole structures*, as shown in Figure 19 (see also Probst, 1987).

During a period of 'inexorable growth', Hewlett-Packard was able to develop an early warning system using its existing human resources. The system gives the organization timely indications of impending crises and opportunities (Deiss and Dierolf, 1991). Unfortunately, an achievement of this kind is the exception.

Organizations can use slack resources to look for new behaviours, and to experiment with possible future scenarios. Looking for problems often takes precedence over looking for opportunities. However, even companies which

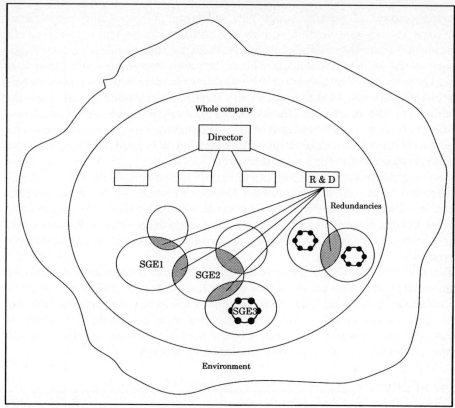

Figure 19 Redundant structures and redundancy within structures.

have the structure described above, and are therefore in a position to look for new opportunities or apply innovative solutions, often fail to take advantage of this potential. Research has repeatedly shown that only a small number of organizations make use of their slack resources or their internal structures so as to open up new opportunities or deal with future complexities. In practice, success and plenty are much more likely to lead to sluggishness, persistence in existing behaviours, exclusion of new strategies and strengthening of traditions (Hedberg, 1981). Preservation of knowledge is an obstacle to learning; learning damages or destroys the knowledge contained in existing structures. It has long been recognized that success supports everyday routines, at the expense of curiosity, creativity and readiness to change.

Learning can also be triggered by members of the organization (Hedberg, 1981). When members express differing opinions on various matters, they disturb the internal environment. In this way, they can influence decision-makers and cause strategies to be questioned. When there is a change of leadership, the presence of new personalities can bring about a different orientation which affects the whole company. The new leadership may question existing courses of action, adopt new strategic positions and redistribute resources. In such circumstances, new and charismatic leaders at the head of a company are often responsible for changes because they develop fresh strategic visions at the start of their appointment, transmit new values and attempt to apply them within a new structure. Examples of leaders who have developed a new vision and mission statement at the start of their period of office are the presidents of ABB or Oticon. This happened because the new leaders questioned existing behaviours. The dismissal of top management can have the same result, since established behaviours come to be regarded as invalid, and this may also present an opportunity for a new approach.

Learning processes can be triggered not only by the appointment or dismissal of leaders, but by that of any internal bearer of knowledge. If an employee is moved or dismissed, this favours the often salutary process of unlearning; conversely, a new employee may bring in new knowledge. This in turn can lead to the questioning of existing norms, as opinions begin to be expressed and discussed.

Learning can also be triggered by less radical events than dismissals and new appointments. It can be set in motion by the further training of members of the organization, by job rotation and by changes in working relationships. It is also clear that events which precipitate learning and those which precipitate unlearning are closely related and often coincide. Various precipitants can trigger unlearning, and unlearning can lead to learning.

Case study 5

IBM

IBM has been the world's most successful international computer company. Its strong market presence, technological leadership, financial potential and distinct company culture have enabled it to achieve countless triumphs in the eighty years of its existence. However, even IBM has not been able to escape the effects of the profound structural changes in the computer industry, combined with the worldwide recession, the enormous pressure on prices and profit margins, and the trend towards smaller systems. The speed of this change in the computer industry is probably unique, and IBM as an organization must continue to learn, and to make profound changes, if it wishes to maintain its position of leadership and to offer its

customers the best possible solutions. The crisis has called for a radical change of orientation and the development of a new company culture.

In the early 1990s there were several indications of the changes which had already taken place, and the resultant upheaval. The number of factories worldwide fell from 42 to 30, and the production capacity was reduced by 40 per cent, although production itself was actually being increased. Retraining of 75,000 employees took place; 36,000 were moved to customer-oriented positions, 84,000 were taken out of supporting functions and 11,000 supervisory positions were removed. Since 1986, total personnel has been reduced by more than 100,000, to less than 300,000. The costs of restructuring in 1992 alone imposed a burden of US$ 11 billion on the businesses' financial results; this was one of the reasons why the company as a whole was in the red.

The computer industry is continuously experiencing profound changes involving three factors: the customer, technology and competition. Customers are no longer just looking for the best value for money in terms of hardware, software and service. They want ready-made solutions for their business, and they want to know where the added value of these solutions lies. Since the computer made its entry into the business world, technological development has brought enormous improvements in price and performance, to the tune of 20--25 per cent per year on average. Twenty-five years ago, IBM had barely 1,000 competitors; now, it has more than 50,000. In the face of stiff competition, only those who are quick to find new market niches and new business areas can survive. Where IBM lacks the knowledge which it needs to do this, it forms partnerships and alliances.

These turbulent times have served as a *trigger* for organizational learning in IBM. The company recognized that the path it was following and its existing structures had lost their validity, and that a completely new kind of architecture was needed. To put this into practice, IBM has had to undergo several learning processes.

In 1993 the company had new ideas, new freedoms, fresh vigour and a new market orientation. It also had common rules of play and a shared roof, and it continued to abide by its proven principles. IBM in 1993 consisted of nine production and development units, organized according to product groups, and four international marketing companies, organized by regions. The thirteen 'companies within a company' were independent and individually responsible for their business actions. The production companies were free to decide where the best business opportunities lay, and to develop their products according to market demands. Their main customers were the IBM marketing companies, but they could also sell to third parties, who then offered products under their own name. Conversely, the marketing companies could use the products of other companies, if this offered a better way of making up a total solution for a customer. Each of the thirteen units determined its own strategy and goals. The Corporation itself monitored the whole structure, and retained responsibility for company strategy and principles. Both for IBM and for the customers, these developments represented a radical change and amounted to the introduction of the free market into the company. The external changes triggered the company to learn, to change and to adapt itself to new circumstances. The learning was primarily reconstructive, since basic premises were questioned, which led to a new framework for action (*IBM Transformator*, 1993).

Case study 6

Hewlett-Packard

In 1988, Hewlett-Packard had 87,000 employees and sold a range of more than 10,000 products for measurement and data processing. It had a turnover of

US$ 9.8 billion. Hewlett-Packard Germany, the largest overseas branch of the company, grew by 20 per cent annually between 1968 and 1988, from a turnover of DM 78 million to DM 2.8 billion.

Hewlett-Packard had an unusual motto: 'Tomorrow's world will probably be no better and no worse than today's, but at least we know it will be different' (Deiss and Dierolf, 1991). Even in times of apparently unlimited growth, the company wanted to draw people's attention to the fact that success in the past is no guarantee of success in the future. Hewlett-Packard Germany therefore launched a project to examine its central information system and to prepare it to meet the future.

The first step was to take stock of all the planning, control and information systems in use. These were checked using appropriate instruments. The company discovered duplications and internal contradictions between data. It also found that although many different kinds of data were stored, they were mainly of a technical nature. The available information related mainly to the past.

Starting from these findings, a project team was set up to develop an integrated early warning system. The aim was to develop a system which would show up probable future conflicts and dependencies, and which would contain early-warning indicators. It would also be flexible, simple and transparent. This was to be achieved by

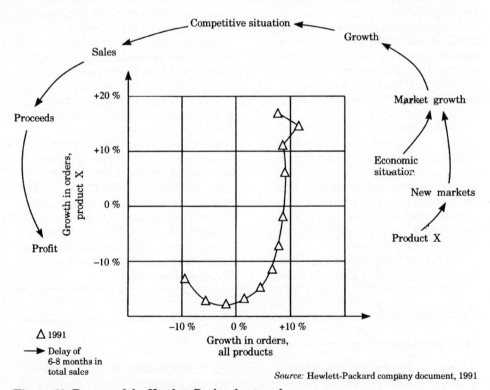

Source: Hewlett-Packard company document, 1991

Figure 20 Extract of the Hewlett-Packard network.

means of 'network thinking', which allows complex problems to be viewed from different angles and comprehensive networks to be developed.

The search for early-warning indicators within Hewlett-Packard revealed a wide variety of relevant influences and relationships. These were used to work backwards from the goal, analyzing situations which might come about in the future. The team was looking for signals. Sales figures were investigated as a possible early warning sign. However, since sales are preceded by orders, it was thought that a detailed analysis of orders might provide an alternative basis. The calculation of trends and study of product groups or

customer segments proved to be sources of information on future developments.

Records of orders were therefore chosen as the basis of the early warning system, and they were investigated in greater detail. An interesting correlation was soon found between short-term growth in components and long-term growth in other products. The components market represents only a very small part of total turnover, but it nevertheless provides a good early warning signal which helps the company to act rather than react (Figure 20). Based on existing figures on incoming orders for components, future predictions could be made for the

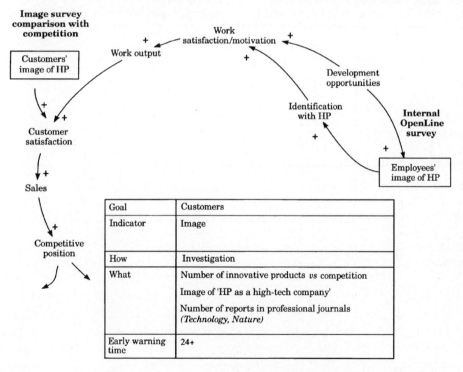

Goal	Customers
Indicator	Image
How	Investigation
What	Number of innovative products *vs* competition
	Image of 'HP as a high-tech company'
	Number of reports in professional journals *(Technology, Nature)*
Early warning time	24+

Source: Hewlett-Packard; *cf.* Probst and Gomez, 1991

Figure 21 Early-warning indicators at Hewlett-Packard.

number of product orders.

Another early warning indicator which Hewlett-Packard developed in detail was the image of the organization held by customers and by employees. Plans were made to measure the image in various ways, for example by employee surveys, number of reports in professional journals. The image signal provides an early-warning signal for a variety of social and economic changes (Figure 21).

In 1989/90, Hewlett-Packard decided to make cuts in personnel and to assemble various product packages. The decisions were made in response to a number of signals and scenarios. The company also intensified market development and customer orientation. As a result, Hewlett-Packard entered the 1990s as a successful company, which was an exception in the information technology market.

This example shows that successful companies which have sufficient resources or redundancy in the areas of structure or personnel can be in a position to learn. Hewlett-Packard used the resources at its disposal to introduce learning processes during a period of growth. The presence of slack, which can provide a basis for organizational learning, permitted Hewlett-Packard to build up an early warning system as part of its problem-solving capacity. The early warning system involves analysis of strengths and weaknesses, which leads to continuous comparison of various dimensions. Companies are thus able to adapt rapidly if deviations from the path leading to goal fulfilment are discovered.

WORKSHEET IV

Analysis of factors which trigger learning

■ In what areas do we have slack resources which could be better used for learning processes?

	Description of resources	Possible use for learning processes
■ **Potentials** – Employee potential – Financial potential – R & D potential – Customer relations – Performance potential – Information technology – Logistics – Potential for cooperation – Market potential – Raw materials – –		
■ **Structural redundancies** – Finance – Human resources – Marketing – Service – –		
■ **Early warning systems/ elements** – Social area – Financial area – Technological area – Performance area – –		

WORKSHEET IV (continued)

■ Possible turbulence or crises which could trigger learning processes

	Description of situation	Possible consequences	Learning needs
– Falling turnover figures – Leadership conflicts – Personnel fluctuations – Change of leadership – Restructuring – Problems with the product – Changes in structure of clientele – Market developments – – – –			

■ What factors are of particular significance in your company today?

– – –

Source: based on Argyris and Schön, 1978

5

Who are the agents of organizational learning?

Having looked at the factors which trigger organizational learning, we now move on to ask who are its agents. We have already argued that it is the interactions between the individual and the organization that are vital: neither the individual nor the organization should be regarded as the dependent variable in the relationship. Our aim in this chapter is to identify the agents of organizational learning. In Chapter 7, we take a closer look at the active part played by individuals, elites and groups in initiating learning processes.

The question of the agents of learning has generally been approached in one of two ways. The first approach identifies organizational learning as learning by individuals within the organization. This is based on the assumption that people and their cognitive capacities, values and motivations are the *agents* of the learning process. The second approach attempts to explain organizational learning through identifying processes at a level other than that by individuals. This approach views organizations as having storage systems which form a link between the internal and external environments (Figure 22).

1 Individuals as agents

Models which equate organizational learning with learning by individuals draw attention to the fact that organizations cannot have quasi-individual cognitive processes, and that only people are capable of learning by means of mental activity (Jelinek, 1979). Approaches which make individuals central to

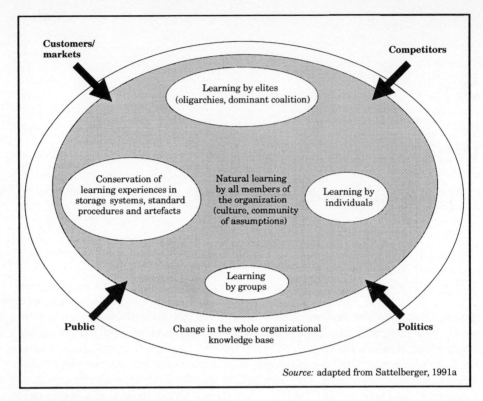

Figure 22 Learning by different agents.

organizational learning focus on people and their motives, interests and values. These motives etc. form the basis of cognitive processes which result in learning. Models based on individual learning emphasize the personal component in behavioural change and neglect the collective aspect.

Human communication is a specific expression of the collective learning of individuals: through dialogue, individual experiences become intersubjective reality, and are collectively communicable and changeable. First, communication enables individuals to question their basic premises or reflect on their theories of action; secondly, it enables them to apply the knowledge which they have gained to particular problems. Discussions between individuals lead to the development of a collective view of reality within the organization. Individuals contribute the fruits of their individual learning; however, these are of no value without discussion, argument and the process of reaching a consensus.

2 Elites as agents

Another form of learning which may take place within organizations is learning by elites. 'Organizational learning thus becomes that process in the organization through which members of the dominant coalition develop, over time, the ability to discover when organizational changes are required and what changes can be undertaken which they believe will succeed' (Duncan and Weiss, 1979: 78).

Learning may take place through a representative elite or the dominant coalition. This may consist of the directors or other leaders of the organization, or of powerful members of particular groups. For the purposes of this theory, organizations are regarded as oligarchic systems in which a dominant coalition emerges and rules the organization. Against this background, learning and power are perceived as being closely related. There is also the implication that the knowledge of the powerful has the greatest chance of determining organizational decisions and changes. This is especially clear when charismatic leaders take over an organization and change existing structures, question values or formulate new goals. A change of leadership often functions as a trigger for organizational learning, since basic changes are made which for years had not even been contemplated. In this way the leadership, or the elite, can be an agent of learning.

3 Groups as agents

As life grows increasingly complex, it becomes more difficult for individual executives to be the agents of learning for an entire organization and to guide the whole learning process. In many different areas of company life we now find self-organized groups which exert a major influence on decision-making. This means that the agents of learning may include not only a dominant coalition but also subgroups of all kinds. Various groups such as political alliances, innovation teams or even whole functional areas can be vehicles for learning. Specific management levels or management areas can exert a decisive influence in both horizontal and vertical directions on the learning of an organization. Finally, the agents of learning do not need to be powerful; they can also be creative groups such as network teams within the firm. Innovation groups, for instance, produce ideas for modifying the rules of the game. Their suggestions are considered when critical decisions are made, and subsequently enter the collective knowledge base. A vital role is played by those members of the organization who are the first to act according to the new rules, thus paving the way for them to be institutionalized for the whole organization.

Self-organizing groups in particular strategic areas contribute to changes in knowledge by redefining their own context and sphere of action. Inter-disciplinary project teams with members taken from many different areas place their knowledge at the disposal of the organization. Internal groups such as these stimulate exchanges which generate new knowledge. When this knowledge is made accessible to the organization in the form of rules of play and instructions for action, the teams have initiated the learning process and served as its agents. An important factor in changing and improving the knowledge base is the process of reaching an agreement amongst all the groups or individuals in the system. Members of the organization bring about organizational learning by changing knowledge which is shared by most of the members. Organizational learning occurs as a result of changes in commonly shared values and assumptions by the majority of the members of the organization. This knowledge is objectivized — or made impersonal — within the organization, since it becomes common property. A shared view of reality contains the objectivized assumptions of the members of the organization about behaviours and their consequences. The process of reaching agreement amongst the members of the organization leads to basic changes in the frame of reference, or, in other words, to organizational learning.

Groups are important agents to learning since a number of individuals may overcome barriers to learning. According to Garratt (1990), when groups work as a team they should have the following characteristics to enable them to overcome barriers to learning:

■ They should have a specified role.
■ They should be allowed the space and time to reflect upon their organizational reality.
■ They should use individually developed strengths.
■ They should acknowledge that learning is a continuing process.

Teams that have these characteristics have been recognized as critical agents of organizational learning.

4 Social systems as agents

There are other theories of organizational learning which do not focus on groups or individuals as agents of learning. Theories of this kind are mainly concerned with changes in the organization itself, i.e. with the collection and standardization of learning experiences in rules, artefacts or systems. Organizations are regarded as having storage systems containing hypotheses by means of which links can be established between the internal and external environments. These represent the organization's knowledge or memory, and enable it to store knowledge and continue to process it without the aid of individual members (Figure 23).

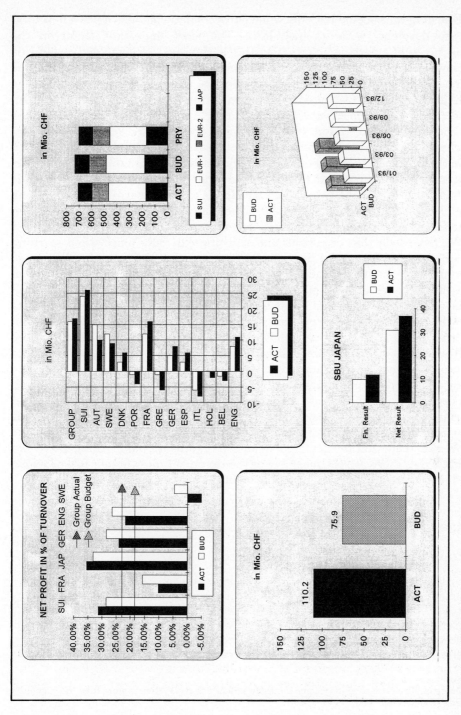

Figure 23 'Dashboard' as storage system.

Learning thus occurs not only when parts combine but also when a new total system develops, with its own laws. The most important factor in the appearance of emergent[1] characteristics is the level of complexity, and this cannot be deduced from the parts. The behaviour of a group, for example, is more complex than can be deduced from a study of its members. When individual parts are restricted, which means restricting their level of freedom, a new whole can appear which is qualitatively different from the sum of the individual parts. At system level, learning processes are determined by two mechanisms, namely structures and processes. According to Willke (1991), structures permit the system to use only certain combinations of elements; processes permit the system to control the order of combination of elements. It is thus possible for novelty to appear within the system. Learning processes lead to a change in the organization itself, since the standardization of learning in structures and processes constitutes deep rather than superficial change.

We have seen that organizational learning can take place when learning experiences are conserved in structures and processes. These changes in the organization can take place when learning experiences are formalized in procedures, rules or programmes, thus permitting learning to be transferred independently of individual members of the organization. The culture and its associated values also serve as a storage system because they contain instructions and patterns of behaviour. The organizational memory, stored partly on computers, contains informal or formal rules and information for the future, which enrich the knowledge base.

By using and modifying the store of knowledge, and continuing to develop it, the organization can increase its knowledge base and facilitate organizational learning. Learning results not only from the actual storage of knowledge but also from the modification of the knowledge base.

We see, then, that the principal agents of organizational learning are of two kinds. First, there are the members of the organization, whether few or many; secondly, there are storage systems used in the organization.

Case study 7

Group project in Allianz Insurance

The Allianz group of the German insurance company Allianz Insurance ran a project in which a group learning process was used to introduce new leadership principles (von Hof, 1991). Internal working groups in the Allianz Insurance consist of the group leader, his or her deputy, and about twenty employees. These groups deal mostly with the outside world and are in contact with customers and insurance representatives. A changing business

---

[1] 'Emergent' is a term used in systems theory to indicate that a system is more than the sum of its parts (Willke, 1991: 148).

environment and the speed of technological change have brought marked changes to the work done by these groups and to the ways in which they work as a team. As automation increased, group leaders lost their position of omniscience and omnipotence, and some control over the workflow. This meant that they no longer had to perform some of their traditional tasks, but at the same time, they acquired others, for example they became responsible for the social cohesion of the groups. Changing circumstances transformed the groups from 'work-processing units' into 'problem-solving units' at the interfaces between the business and customers, and between the business and representatives.

In response to these changes, a project was launched to initiate discussion of leadership. Leadership principles were developed in a collective learning process embracing all those concerned. The learning process was to have the following features:

■ The leader, working with his or her group, was to be the agent of the learning process.
■ The initial situation, together with existing problems, agreements and disagreements on values, should be clear and comprehensible to all.
■ Opportunities and difficulties arising from the principles should be made clear.
■ Enthusiasm for action should be applied and encouraged.
■ The members of the group should work together on suggested solutions.
■ There should be a consensus-building process.

The method used in the project was the 'discussion market'. Each leader held a discussion with his or her group members; the subject was teamwork in relation to the leadership principles. This activity took place at every level. To help the group leaders in steering the discussions, a guideline was produced; this contained advice and methodological aids (see Figure 24).

The results were collected into a discussion guideline, based on the principles that members should:

■ Be personally prepared for the discussion
■ Follow the development of the discussion, and help to guide it
■ Formulate measures
■ Keep appointments
■ Make sure that the discussions happen
■ Continue the discussion if necessary

After the discussion guideline had been tried out in the training department, it was implemented throughout the organization. Criticisms and positive comments were made, problem areas were tackled. When the discussions were evaluated, it emerged that they had in fact amounted to more than a marathon exercise in self-analysis; they had turned into a group-supported continuing process of interactive learning.

The preliminary stage of the group project led to improved upward communication in the working groups. The aim was to establish self-regulating processes in dynamic equilibrium; these, it was hoped, would lead to creative solutions. The approach helped the group leaders to become more aware of their role, and facilitated agreement on the functions of group members. It was also valuable in settling conflicts and developing models for problem-solving. The whole exercise resulted in organizational learning, the agents being

Agreement on aims	■ Formulate aims and express in measurable terms ■ What aims can we influence most?

Problem landscape	■ Enter problems on map (formulate as problems)
	■ Compile contexts of problems
	  – What information do we still need?
	  – What other groups are affected?

Starting-points for action	■ Are there vicious circles? ■ Which problems have arrows leading from them? (causes)
Strategy and measures	■ What measures are appropriate here? ■ What measures can be combined? ('multiple use') ■ What undesired effects could there be? ■ What are the signals which will enable us to recognize success and failure?
Initial and subsequent steps	■ Where shall we start? (favourable opportunities, prospects for success)
Reflection, evaluation	After each phase: ■ Evaluate the measures ■ Identify the 'signals' ■ Effects of others (self-image, image of others)

Source: von Hof, 1991: 270

Figure 24 Guideline for groups.

the group and its members. Changes were made to the common frame of reference, new values and norms were established and new behaviours emerged. The primary agents for the development of the leadership principles were the top management, i.e. the elite. However, the leadership principles in themselves would have been useless if the realities had not been discussed with the rest of the people involved. The notion that only the leaders were capable of improving motivation, teamwork and leadership was soon discarded in favour of a systematic examination of the whole situation. The groups emerged as the real agents of the learning process, and they developed a network of shared norms. These were then used as a basis for communication and teamwork.

WORKSHEET V

Record of critical agents of learning process

- Who are the critical agents of change in your company?
- Which employees or groups should be supported so that their knowledge and innovations can be made available to the whole organization?
- Which persons are responsible for putting new ideas into practice, so that new concepts can be established in procedures and rules?

Critical agents of learning	Support needed	Responsible for implementation
Individuals		
Elite		
Groups		
Systems		

6

What are the barriers to learning?

We now turn to the question of why organizational learning does not happen much more often, and why it is not, in fact, a continuous process. What are the factors which impede learning or prevent it from taking place?

We argued in a previous chapter that stable knowledge structures can impede learning since learning disturbs or destroys knowledge in its existing form. The existing knowledge base must undergo structural change if organizational learning is to take place. However, organizations tend to resist change, since the success of a particular strategy confirms the validity of the existing procedures. This means that if an organization wishes to change, it must view its internal storage systems as an enemy (Hedberg, 1981). Argyris (1985) states that success strengthens the organization's theories of action and hampers the process of unlearning.

1 The difficulty of unlearning

Unlearning is the process by which knowledge is erased from the memory. Hedberg (1981) describes this process as a series of 'little deaths' at the micro-level, since old structures and ways of thinking must be removed from the repertoire in order to make room for new ones. Unlearning makes it possible for new knowledge to be accepted, and for old structures to be changed or removed. However, since success tends to preserve existing structures and behaviours, it would appear that there must be serious obstacles to unlearning. Members of the organization — including the leaders — typically lack the means and the opportunity to free themselves from their immediate environment and promote change. Larger organizations fritter away their resources in internal power struggles instead of using them to bring about fundamental changes in behaviour. Decision-makers and advisers repeatedly find that organizations resist learning because they do not want to change old knowledge structures.

The process of unlearning is characterized by a change in knowledge structures. These structures can be described in terms of cognitive patterns. The patterns may dissolve either when old events are seen as having new outcomes, or when the event itself is perceived differently, as something new or changed (Watzlawick *et al.*, 1974; Postman and Underwood, 1973). In the former situation, there is the perception that new information does not fit, so the connection between event and outcome is broken. This means that further links, for example the existing theory of action, the philosophy or the norms, must also be sacrificed (Hedberg, 1981). In the latter case, i.e. when the event itself is perceived differently, it is this changed perception which leads to a break in the connection between event and outcome. The cognitive pattern can then be 'restructured' (Watzlawick *et al.*, 1974).

Unlearning takes time, and makes demands on other resources. Organizations generally fail to recognize the full importance of learning new things and unlearning old ones. When the company is entering a transitional phase — moments of disorientation — it must retain the trust of the outside world and of its customers so that a constructive new phase can begin.

Organizational learning is most frequently triggered by factors such as falling turnover, rising costs, financial deficit, public criticism or changes of leadership. These factors intensify the search for something new and confirm the insufficiency of the the firm's capacity for action and problem-solving ability. When old philosophies are declared inadequate and are discarded, organizations can replace their old theories of action with new ones, thus clearing the way for new philosophies, programmes and concepts.

Unfortunately, not all organizations are in a position to put these ideas into practice. First, it requires sufficient resources, for example enough time. These resources are often unavailable because the firm is about to be acquired or has other pressing issues. Secondly, there is a significant danger that the phase of disorientation will be accompanied by uncertainty and a leadership vacuum; this makes the reorientation phase even more difficult. Finding the right balance between the organization's ability to preserve its knowledge structures and its ability to forget is a determinant of future success. However, it is often emphasized that few organizations achieve this difficult balancing act.

2 Obstacles to unlearning

In our opinion, the following factors constitute *critical barriers to learning*:

■ Organizational defensive patterns
■ Norms, privileges and taboos
■ Information disorders

2.1 Organizational defensive patterns

According to Argyris and Schön (1978), the failure of many firms to achieve a balance between the preservation of existing knowledge structures and the necessary degree of unlearning can be explained by the existence of 'limited learning systems'. These systems conceal errors — at least for the time being — by introducing inconsistencies and making attempts at disguise. Such tactics lead to paradoxes, dilemmas and inconsistent actions and can be called organizational defensive patterns.

The 'Mercury story' told by Argyris and Schön (1978) is a striking example of these mechanisms at work. At the beginning of the 1970s, the management of an organization had arrived at a clear definition of an internal organizational problem. The structure of the organization was highly centralized, which meant that the management of business units was overstretched and unable to pay sufficient attention to strategically important decisions. The obvious solution was decentralization, and appropriate measures were put into effect. Senior managers approved this new structure. Management's theories in use now included the concept of decentralization with central control over divisional results. Managers of divisions were given the freedom to put their own ideas into practice. Central control was to take the form of agreements with the divisions on objectives. However, the managers of the divisions had built up mechanisms which enabled them to avoid having to reveal their actions, thus protecting various freedoms which they had previously established for themselves. Ultimately, this led to inconsistencies between the theories in action of top management and those of divisional managers. The divisional managers' protective mechanisms consisted in following these rules:

■ Avoid direct personal contact and public discussion of sensitive issues.
■ Control the public discussions of issues, so that negative feelings do not arise.
■ Assess the situation and form your own opinion — but keep it quiet.

Theoretically, the inconsistency between the theories in use and the official theories of action should have triggered organizational learning. However, as Argyris (1990) points out, other mechanisms were involved which hindered learning.

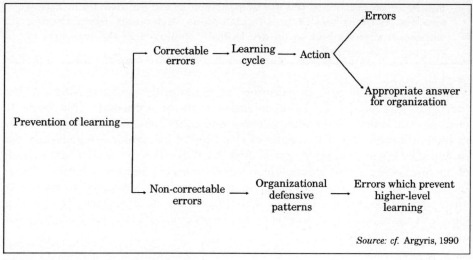

Figure 25 Limited learning systems.

- **Skilled incompetence**
- **Organizational defensive routines**
- **'Fancy footwork' and 'malaise'**

These processes are *organizational defensive patterns,* and they are the main barriers to higher-level learning.

Figure 25 shows how errors in theories of action are concealed rather than exposed. Concealment then leads to further errors. We shall now describe these processes in more detail.

2.1.1 Skilled incompetence

From their earliest childhood, people learn how to react to painful or threatening circumstances so as not to lose control of the situation. The behaviours which they learn are transformed into theories of action which are used for coping with everyday life. According to Argyris (1990), people dislike losing control over their actions, and like to be praised when they have done well. When a threatening or painful situation arises, there is always the danger of losing control or of not being praised. Most people therefore follow a theory of action which says that they must stay in control, and remain master of the situation. To stay in control, they often have to tell lies, or invent stories, so as not to lose face. The mechanisms they use to stay in control or to conceal painful and threatening situations have been termed 'skilled incompetence' (Argyris, 1985; 1990).

> **Skilled incompetence is the use of strategies based on theories of action aimed at avoiding loss of face. Explanations, distortions, inexactitudes, omissions, excuses and so on are skilfully deployed in the interests of keeping what one has.**

Problems which are threatening or potentially embarrassing to the individual are countered by a defensive style of argument. This leads to misunderstandings, distortions, silences and concealments, and thus to errors in human interaction. The results of this kind of behaviour are generally not intended by the individual (Argyris, 1990: 21). Skilled incompetence is the result of unconsciously adroit moves which are ultimately counterproductive. These tactics are used because our behaviour is already programmed to switch to automatic protective mechanisms which guide our daily actions. The process generally takes no more than a fraction of a second, so it is usually unconscious and difficult to control.

2.1.2 Defensive routines

Because skilled incompetence is part of our everyday behaviour, it becomes an organizational norm. It is therefore regarded as rational and realistic.

> **Mechanisms used automatically to protect individuals and groups within the organization from painful and threatening situations are termed 'defensive routines'.**

Defensive routines are likely to lead to errors in the behaviour of individuals and groups. The following behaviours show defensive routines at work (Argyris, 1990: 43):

■ Bypassing errors and ignoring the bypassing
■ Making the bypass undiscussable
■ Making its undiscussability undiscussable

These mechanisms limit the likelihood of existing structures breaking down. Even the attempt to prevent the mechanisms from operating can strengthen these structures. The phenomenon is also described as a 'shadow economy', because the attempt to cure the illness only makes it worse, or has the potential to cause new illnesses. The comparison with a shadow economy or mafia shows why organizational defensive routines are so difficult to break down. Although the shadow economy does not officially exist, it lives and thrives underground. Official denial of its existence creates conditions in which it can spread. A shadow economy is to be found in most organizations and is generally regarded as untouchable either because attempts at change usually just make things worse or because individuals are not prepared to take the consequences of 'stirring up' the problem. The mechanisms are therefore stable t which renders unlearning exceedingly difficult.

2.1.3 Fancy footwork and malaise

Another kind of mechanism inherent in limited learning systems is descr ̣ ̣ ̣y Argyris (1990) as fancy footwork. This refers to behaviours which enable people to be blind towards inconsistencies in their own actions or to make others responsible for them. They embrace a variety of strategies for concealing the truth.

Fancy footwork means the use of all mechanisms which rely on protective, defensive argumentation to deny mistakes or to conceal them from the people who made them and from those in authority.

Examples of this kind of behaviour can be found within groups who try ineffectively to deal with precarious issues. The main reason for their ineffectiveness is usually unawareness of individuals about the group behaviour. A cycle of concealment and denial mechanisms is at work; and this cycle is difficult to break. This prevents the kind of unlearning that we have described. The group usually starts to suffer from an indefinable malaise. People feel uncomfortable, keep their distance and are aware of the presence of dishonesty, rejection, reticence, etc. This may be described as illness in the system.

Because of individual and group-specific behaviours, these processes are often encountered and become part of the culture. They can only be overcome by attacking the causes; treatment of the symptoms is not enough.

The syndrome which includes skilled incompetence, defensive routines and fancy footwork is described as malaise, because it is an unpleasant illness which leads to high costs and waste of energy for the company.

The barriers to learning which we have just described may be found in one form or another in most organizations, in varying degrees of severity. The mechanisms of skilled incompetence, organizational defensive routines and fancy footwork together with the resultant malaise, constitute organizational defensive patterns, and are the chief barriers to organizational learning (Figure 26).

These behavioural patterns occur in most companies just as they do in families. They develop as a result of attempts to deal with painful or threatening situations. They can be traced back to theories in use and social values learned in childhood.

Organizational learning

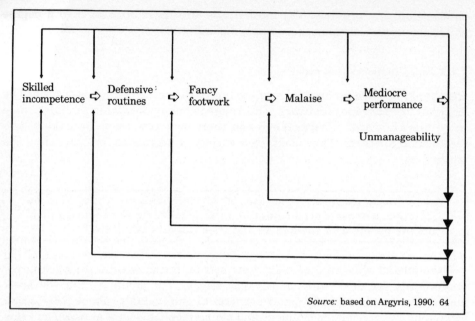

Figure 26 Organizational defensive patterns.

2.2 Norms, privileges and taboos as barriers to learning

We have described how social systems contain various fundamental sources of resistance which make unlearning extremely difficult. One source of resistance is to be found in norms or habitual patterns of behaviour. Every organization is characterized by particular behaviours such as working arrangements, clothing, forms of address, consumption behaviour and recognized ways of organizing leisure time. These mould the ways in which people work together and they determine people's expectations. Because these norms are shared by a large number of people, they are not easy to change, and so they hamper new developments. If someone dares to deviate from the norms, the result is usually public rejection of the individual concerned or of the whole group. Norms can only be changed if they are considered in the total context of relationships. Parts can take on unintended characteristics because of their relationships to the whole; this means that they must be approached in the context of the totality. Components of institutional change are not islands in themselves; they are embedded in the whole network.

'Killer phrases' are an example of behaviour patterns which can cause resistance in internal company communication, and thus hinder comprehensive organizational change (Bloch et al., 1986; Probst, 1993). Remarks such as the following are hostile to creativity and communication:

- That'll never work.
- I do have other things to do.
- If it ain't broke, don't fix it.
- Everybody does not like that.
- It's different for us.
- But that's not the point.
- *How* long have you been here?
- I haven't got time! Let's wait and see.
- It's not my decision.
- Good idea! Let me have it in writing sometime.

Privileges and taboos are also obstacles to learning. Members of an organization are reluctant to give up their financial advantages and their privileges. They use their power to keep them. Taboos are a form of resistance because morals and customs are extremely difficult to change. It is not surprising that taboos are undiscussable, because they relate to areas which are perceived as painful and threatening. This becomes clear when we consider the position of women in society. We accept women as captains of aircraft and as business and political leaders, but it may be some time before we see a woman as a bishop, as president of a board of directors, or as prime minister of Italy (though the exception proves the rule).

2.3 Information disorders

According to Pautzke (1989), organizational learning is limited in part by the information processing capacity of the organization. *Information disorders* are regarded as obstacles to learning. Pautzke lists the following kinds of information disorders:

- Structural information disorders
- Doctrinal information disorders
- Psychological information disorders

A structural information disorder is present when information is blocked or distorted because of hierarchy, specialization or centralization. These factors can prevent decision-makers from having access to all the information they need. Figure 27 shows the potential faults in an organization with a traditional structure. The different management levels are cut off from each other — there are functional barriers or 'operational islands'. As a result, neither top management nor divisional managers can make well-founded decisions.

Doctrinal information disorders such as slogans or mottos distort information and allow a picture to be created which does not correspond with multiple viewpoints. This in turn gives rise to a selective approach to

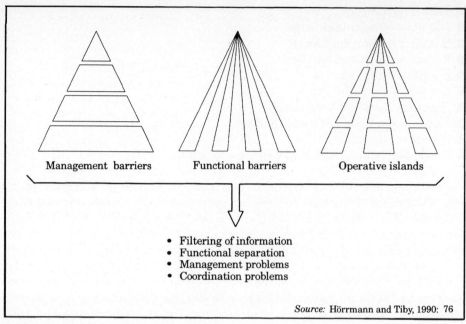

Figure 27 Structural information disorders: structural faults in traditional forms of organization.

information: certain kinds of information are favoured, which means that decision-makers do not have the full picture.

Psychological information disorders also limit the information processing capacity of the organization. Individuals prefer consonant cognitive structures to dissonant ones; this need for cognitive harmony leads to the suppression of dissonant information. Unpleasant information is disregarded.

> **Organizational defensive patterns, norms, privileges, taboos and information disorders all hinder the learning process and make unlearning difficult.**

In the next chapter, we consider factors which facilitate organizational learning and which can disrupt organizational defensive patterns. We look at circumstances which favour the questioning of norms and values, and which promote an adequate flow of information.

Case study 8 ———————————————

The Challenger disaster

The disaster which befell the Challenger space shuttle in 1986 shows how defensive routines operating throughout an organization can prevent learning from taking place (see Argyris, 1990: 37ff.).

NASA had known for years that the O-rings on the launching rocket were unreliable in cold weather. The rings had consistently shown signs of erosion following flights at temperatures below 61°F (16°C). The evening before the Challenger flight, two of the engineers responsible for the development and production of the launching rockets and the O-rings expressed doubts about the timing of the launch, in view of the low temperature. Their doubts were overruled by management.

Prior to the launch, one of the engineers responsible for the O-rings had put his worries in writing to NASA. Another wrote a memo that started with the word 'HELP', and ended with: 'This is a red flag'. These memos never arrived at the appropriate place. On the morning of the launch, the two engineers of the producers of the O-rings once more drew NASA's attention to the fact that the rings were not guaranteed safe at temperatures below below 50°F (10°C). The outside temperature on the morning of the disaster was 36°F (2°C). Nevertheless, the flight took off at 11.38, and disaster followed.

The investigation showed that the concerns of the engineers had not been taken seriously by their superiors because there had been no problems during previous flights. The safety of flights in the past was used to predict the safety of flights in the future. Moreover, postponement of the flight would have had grave financial consequences. The warnings were therefore dismissed, because 'the shuttle has flown nineteen times and has come back nineteen times'.

Another problem was that NASA had interpreted the doubts expressed by the engineers differently. The manager of the launch had the impression that the engineers were worried, but not that they were suggesting a postponement of the flight. His deputy, however, thought that the engineers were strongly opposed to any take-off and that they were arguing for a postponement to another date.

After the engineers had had their concerns rejected by NASA on several occasions, they stopped putting them forward because they thought that nobody was going to listen to them anyway. At a final meeting before the flight, the engineers were asked again if there were any problems. They kept quiet, and their silence was interpreted as agreement by the producers' management. The disastrous launch went ahead.

Both NASA and the engineers used organizational defensive mechanisms. Because of the financial implications, NASA did not want to take the engineers' doubts seriously, so they looked for arguments to support the launch. Even when they were told about the O-rings (engineers' letters and safety regulations on outside temperature), they still argued in favour. A further problem was that the NASA managers did not have an opportunity to discuss their varying interpretations of the engineers' warnings.

The engineers for their part stopped

expressing their anxieties because they thought nobody would listen. By remaining silent when the final decision was made, they in effect sanctioned the launch, even though they were aware of the possible consequences. They used an organizational defensive pattern as a means of escape. This took the form of group pressure, or 'group think' (Whyte, 1989; Esser *et al.*, 1989; Janis, 1972).

The Challenger disaster illustrates the effects of the defensive routines and other defensive mechanisms which were employed not only before the launch of the space shuttle but also after the accident investigation. Neither the state commission nor the engineers' employer identified the central role played by defensive routines. The engineers were sacked because they provided evidence to the commission, and were thus punished for their justified anxieties. NASA then set up an even more comprehensive and rigorous set of safety rules to guard against human error.

In the case of the Challenger disaster, higher-level learning processes did not take place, because the underlying norms and values were not questioned. The authorities tried to improve safety simply by improving the rules. No basic analysis of behaviour was undertaken; but it is only when old behaviours and cognitive patterns are put aside that new points of view can be considered and new interpretations made. This permits higher-level learning to take place.

WORKSHEET VI

Force field analysis

Groups and organizations develop lifestyles, behaviours, procedures and organizational forms which have a tendency to stagnate. All forces which contribute to the stability of the individual or of social systems can also be regarded as forces of resistance to change. A determined and energetic innovator would see them as obstacles. Seen in a wider perspective, forces which tend to create, preserve or reinstate a balance are welcome; they ensure the continued survival of character, intelligent action, institutions, civilization and culture. However, we must then ask, *what we can do when obstacles have to be removed so that change and learning can take place?* If the resistance can be neutralized or reversed, there will be sufficient innovative strength in the system to set change in motion.

■ **Goals of force field analysis:** To make groups aware of the potential for change and for removing obstacles to learning.

■ **Process**

1. The group as a whole defines the problem it wishes to tackle.

2. The group defines and formulates the goal in pursuit of which changes have to be made. (The goal should be presented in visual form for all to see, so that every member of the group can identify with it.)

3. The goal is shown with facilitating and obstructing forces summarized in a diagram. Initially, these forces are entered without evaluation. Anything which has been experienced as a help or a hindrance by individuals or by the group counts as a force. The same factor can be entered both as a positive and as a negative force.
   Individual: conflicts within my value system; skills which I have or which I lack.
   Group: presence or absence of communication; lack of agreement.
   Organization: communication systems, time sequences, flow of information, resources, norms, roles, objectives, decision-making processes.
   Society and environment: various value-systems.

4. When the list is complete, the forces are weighted. The weighting process may take the form of discussion, voting or giving the items values on a scale. The use of a scale with values ranging from 0 to 5 (0 = weak force, 5 = very strong force) means that the strongest forces can be identified during group discussions.

5. A plan of action is then produced, containing the following steps:

   (a) Forces are identified which need to be changed, i.e. weakened or strengthened.
   (b) Concrete plans are made with regard to who will do what, when, and with whom, to bring about these changes.
   (c) A time is agreed for checking the plan of action and evaluating the whole process. There ought to be feedback in the meantime.

WORKSHEET VI (continued)

Guidelines for force field analysis

1. Describe the problem
   (a) What is the situation now?
   (b) What should it be?
2. Many problems could be solved if forces for improvement could be activated and/or forces which impede improvement could be weakened. Which are the facilitating and which are the obstructing forces?

Present situation	
Positive forces	Negative forces
→	←
→	←
→	←
→	←
→	←
→	←
→	←

3. Check through the list of positive and negative forces and underline the ones which seem to you to be the most important at present.
4. For each of the negative forces which you have underlined, ask the following questions:
   (a) How has the force arisen (what is behind it)?
   (b) At what point did it appear (when, how)?
   (c) Who triggered it?
   (d) What facilitates its negative effects?

5. Consider how you might weaken or destroy the negative forces which you have underlined. What would you have to do?

■ Brainstorming:
Negative force 1: _____
Ways to weaken or destroy:

–
–
–

Negative force 2: _____
Ways to weaken or destroy:

–
–
–

WORKSHEET VI (continued)

6. Now do the same for the positive forces which you have underlined.

   Positive force 1: _____
   Ways to maintain or strengthen:

   ```
   –
   –
   –
   ```

   Positive force 2: _____
   Ways to maintain or strengthen:

   ```
   –
   –
   –
   ```

7. Underline those measures which seem likely to succeed.

8. State the means which you would need to carry out the measures, and who could make these means available to you.

9. Formulate a reasonable strategy for tackling your problem.

10. Develop measures for checking your success. When must its effectiveness be examined? How does success show? How long does it last? What measures might help to prolong success?

Source: based on Kurt Lewin, 1951

7

Facilitating organizational learning

We now turn from our study of factors which hinder learning to questions which concern all those in management positions: how can organizational learning be initiated, facilitated and supported? What are the instruments, structures and processes which will enable us to establish conditions conducive to learning?

1 Learning profile of the organization

The learning profile of the organization largely determines what measures can actually be taken and which instruments employed to increase the problem-solving capacity of the organization as a social system, or, in other words, to promote organizational learning. The learning profile defines present conditions in the organization with regard to learning; it yields decisive information on the key factors involved. Current conditions are analyzed to provide information on the existing need for learning, the store of knowledge, current forms of learning, possible agents of learning, internal and external factors which trigger learning, and forces which inhibit it (Figure 28).

The learning profile reveals points where support measures might be introduced, and it is a useful way of evaluating organizational defects and potential problems. If current conditions are wrongly assessed, learning processes may fail to materialize and any measures taken may prove fruitless because of failure to create conditions in which learning can take place. There is no point, for example, in introducing network structures into a company

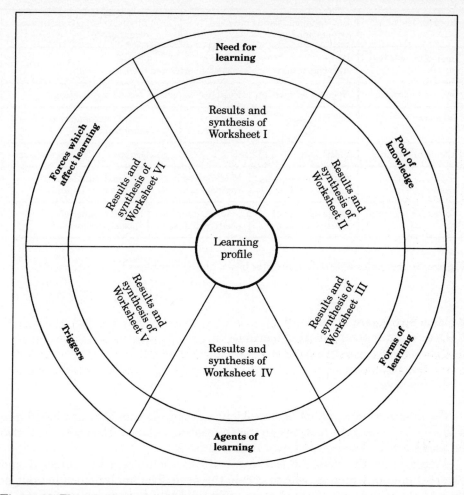

Figure 28 Elements in the learning profile.

which has an informal atmosphere, because there is already plenty of interpersonal contact, and this provides channels for communication and interaction.

Drawing up a learning profile of the organization is an essential first step in promoting organizational learning because it shows the existing position and current strengths and weaknesses of a company. The analysis consists of the following stages:

1. Ascertain the need for learning
2. Analyze knowledge assets
3. Identify forms of learning

Need for learning	Environment (strong outward orientation)		Environment (strong inward orientation)	
Pool of knowledge	Large	Medium	Small	
	Agreement between espoused theories and theories in use			
Forms of learning	Need for adaptation	Need for change	Need for reflection	
Triggers	Crisis mastery		Use of redundancy and free potential	
Agents of learning	Individuals	Elites	Groups	Storage systems
Forces against learning	Large number of negative factors	Medium number of negative factors	Small number of negative factors	
Forces for learning	Large number of positive factors	Medium number of positive factors	Small number of positive factors	

Figure 29 Examples of learning profiles based on the syntheses from worksheets.

4. Identify triggers of learning
5. Determine critical agents of learning
6. Conduct a force field analysis:
   (a) Negative forces
   (b) Positive forces

The information recorded in the various worksheets should be combined into a profile. The general situation can then be seen at a glance. The profile can also be used to chart development over time (Figure 29).

Ascertaining the *need for learning* involves identifying the internal and external factors which appear to create the need. The analysis carried out in Worksheet I shows whether the company is inwardly or outwardly oriented, in terms of the number of internal critical factors identified versus the number of external critical factors.

Analysis of the *pool of knowledge* yields information on the level of knowledge in different categories. It also shows the level of agreement between the official theories of action and the theories in use, and any divergence between them.

Identifying the *forms of learning* permits the investigator to analyze learning processes in his own organization, and thus to determine the level of learning required. There are three decisive criteria for assessing the level of learning: they are *space, time and significance/urgency*. *Space* relates to the depth and breadth of organizational change (are all areas of the firm involved or only some departments?). *Time* means the duration of the learning process (is the change long-term or short-term?). *Significance* means the urgency of the projected learning process, and its attendant risks (is the level of risk high or low?).

Space	Superficial ——— Deep
	Partial ————— Comprehensive
Time	Short-term ——— Long-term
Significance	Low risk ——— High risk

The *triggers* are those factors which set the learning process in motion. If redundancy is present within the organization, creative processes can be set in motion. If the organization is on the brink of crisis, something has to be done in any case.

Identifying the critical *agents* of learning is the first step towards initiating learning processes because it clarifies the issue of who is responsible for bringing about change. The following types of organizational learning can be identified:

■ Representative learning, i.e. learning by individuals on behalf of the organization
■ Learning by elites
■ Learning by groups and subgroups
■ Change of organizational storage systems

Ways in which individuals, elites, groups or storage systems may be supported are recorded in Worksheet V.

The final step is to carry out a force field analysis, which identifies the *forces for and against* change. It identifies both factors which constitute obstacles to learning and factors which facilitate it. The relative numbers of the forces for and against change can then be calculated. Worksheet VI contains a procedure for an initial brainstorming session on how to overcome obstacles to learning and/or strengthen factors which promote it.

The purpose of the learning profile is to evaluate factors which are vital to learning, and thus to create a picture of the existing state of learning processes within the organization. This picture is the framework for further measures, since attempts to promote learning must start from the status quo. The strengths and weaknesses of the organization are revealed, and points are located where change might be introduced.

In the next section, we discuss ways in which learning can be facilitated. Different possible paths towards organizational learning are presented. Which path is chosen depends on the learning profile of the organization.

Worksheet VII

Learning profile

■ **Origin of learning needs**

External environment (outward-looking needs)	Company (inward-looking needs)
☐	☐
☐	☐
☐	☐

■ **Pool of knowledge**

High level of agreement on the following:	Medium level of agreement on the following:	Low level of agreement on the following:
☐	☐	☐
☐	☐	☐
☐	☐	☐

■ **Forms of learning:**

Need for adaptation in:	Need for reconstruction in:	Need for reflection on:
☐	☐	☐
☐	☐	☐
☐	☐	☐

Worksheet VII (continued)

■ Triggers of learning

Crises	Use of redundancy
☐	☐
☐	☐
☐	☐

■ Agents of learning

Individuals	Elites	Groups	Storage systems
☐	☐	☐	☐
☐	☐	☐	☐
☐	☐	☐	☐

■ Forces

Negative forces with		
Strong effect	Medium effect	Weak effect
☐	☐	☐
☐	☐	☐
☐	☐	☐

Positive forces with		
Strong effect	Medium effect	Weak effect
☐	☐	☐
☐	☐	☐
☐	☐	☐

2 Initiation of learning processes

Up to this point, we have concentrated on analyzing the conceptual aspects of organizational learning. We now look at the practical side. In the following section we discuss organizational learning by focusing on the enablers of learning. Measures are mentioned which go beyond surface cosmetics and can lead to real change in the organization's ability to learn.

From the 'learning profile' developed above, we may derive the following basic steps in the management of organizational learning:

- Ascertain the need for learning
- Analyze knowledge assets and forms of learning
- Identify triggers of learning
- Identify agents of learning
- Take steps to overcome barriers to learning
- Develop strategies to create conditions in which learning processes can take place

In addition to these basic steps, we propose a guiding framework, the 'magic square', for organizational learning (Figure 30).

Many models exist which help to systemize organizations (Weisbord, 1976; Nadler and Tushman, 1977; Tichy, 1983; Burke, 1992). Although these models

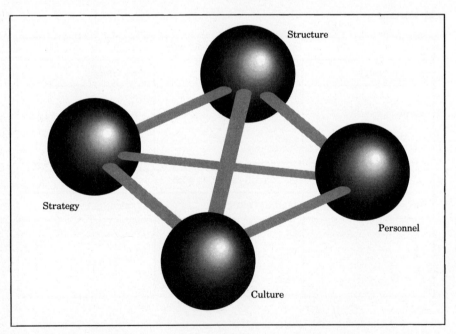

Figure 30 'Magic square'.

emphasize different aspects, they all try to depict the most important elements of organizations. After studying a wide range of models, the overlap became apparent:

- All models seem to view the organization as having a link with the environment. In our model this is shown as *strategy*.
- All models emphasize the importance of structure or design. In our model this is referred to as *structure*.
- Most models consider people within the organization and their inter-relationships to be important. In our model this aspect is summarized under *human resources*.
- In most models, processes within organizations or organizational climate/culture are considered to be important variables. We have summarized this aspect under *culture*.

Although this model may not be a complete picture of what an organization entails, it is the starting point of a systematic approach to organizations. In this book the magic square is used to show the different contexts in which learning can be initiated.

Within this square, the elements influence each other, and their interaction affects the processes of learning and change. The effects of action at any point will spread through the whole organization. It does not matter whether 'structure follows strategy' or 'strategy follows structure': it is argued that wherever action is initiated, learning can be enabled.

The magic square is intended to serve as a theoretical aid to elucidating complex interrelationships. Even though it gives a very simplified view of the whole organization, it is useful as a framework to enable organizational learning. To create a learning organization, we need to start thinking at a number of interrelated points. Without claiming to be comprehensive, we have selected these four points because they seem to be vital elements in guiding organizational learning. Although our choice of these four categories may seem arbitrary, it can be said that they act as enablers in the shaping of processes that will lead to organizational learning.

We regard the following *processes* as vital in the context of organizational learning:

- Strategy development
- Development of culture
- Development of structure
- Human resource development

These processes provide the context for learning. Rather than focus on strategies that help to develop a structure or culture, Chapters 8–11 focus on the process through which learning can be initiated. In other words, rather than learning to develop a strategy, structure, culture or human resources, these different areas are looked at as the contexts in which learning can be initiated.

As Sattelberger, head of human resource development at Lufthansa said: 'If we make learning part of the daily routine; facilitate natural learning processes; open avenues for personal development; establish learning and feedback systems with the environment; structure the processes of planning, strategy development and control as learning experiences for the participants; facilitate the development of culture; and reintegrate learning with work, and teaching with leadership — then we hold the keys to success' (1991a: 22).

We now examine the four contexts of learning in more detail and describe instruments which can be used in each area. To illustrate the different contexts we distinguish between examples and case studies. *Examples* are used in each area to show where action can be taken. In the context of developing a strategy, a wide range of tools can be used to that end including business games, scenario technique, strategic controlling, strategic positioning and environmental scanning. Each chapter which follows contains three examples of tools that help to develop either a strategy, structure, culture or human resources. These examples are then illustrated by a *case study* of a company that has used a specific tool to initiate learning.

8

Learning by developing a strategy

1 The strategic context

Drucker (1980) has described how increasing turbulence in the business world and in the environment has made the task of managing a company a more complex one. Shorter product cycles, new technology and changing values have contributed to a more dynamic business environment, characterized by a greater number of interdependencies. Growing complexity and the speed of change make developments in business and in the environment more difficult to predict. Within this, management should implement strategies which foster long-term, forward-looking thinking and which help the company to influence the future and to act flexibly.

Strategy development is a practical learning exercise in which the future is made a cause of the present (Lessing, 1991). Strategic planning is a process of learning about where the future prospects of a company might lie. The company must examine its potential in great detail. In order to take account of customer needs on the one hand and developments in world markets and technology on the other, strategic planning should be approached both from the bottom up and from the top down. This need for a dual approach implies that numerous people must be involved in the process. Strategic planning is a learning process undertaken by a group of people who get together to think about the future of the company. Involving different members across the organization forms the

Games	Who: All members of the organization Aim: Learning by experience
Scenario technique	Who: Managers (elite) Aim: Learning through analysis
Strategic control	Who: All members of the organization Aim: Learning through analysis

Figure 31 Strategy development as a learning process.

basis of the learning process during which they work together on forecasting and planning the future.

The literature on instruments for strategic planning contains a comprehensive list of strategic planning aids. These are helpful in finding successful strategic positions, and in analyzing the environment, the competition, the market, the company itself and management values. There are classical instruments, for example those which identify strategic business areas; those which analyze the environment, the company or the competition; those which create scenarios, produce portfolios, lead to strategic control, or involve playing business games. However, it is not our purpose here to describe the many strategic planning instruments which are available. We are more concerned with the application of these instruments so that they will trigger a learning process or make a contribution to it. We shall describe three tools for strategy development. These are described for the purpose of clarifying the *learning process*. Learning procedures are indicated which may prove fruitful for the initiation of organizational learning.

Figure 31 shows three types of instrument within the area of strategic management. These instruments are business games (Senge, 1990a; Dörner, 1987); the scenario technique (Ulrich and Probst, 1988; Probst and Gomez, 1991); and strategic control (Pümpin and Geilinger, 1988). We now examine them in more detail.

2 Games in microworlds

People learn best from experience. When someone rides a motorcycle, plays tennis or volleyball, or mends a bicycle, he or she sees the consequences of their actions, and learns from them. In situations of this kind, the learner receives rapid feedback on his or her actions. The person works on a trial-and-error principle, observing his own behaviour and adjusting it as necessary. Prompt feedback means that he can learn from experiences which are close together in time and space (Senge, 1990a, b; Senge and Sterman, 1992).

Games in microworlds give managers an opportunity to learn from real situations. The special feature of this kind of learning is that space and time are compressed, so experimentation, i.e. seeing the consequences of one's actions and learning from them, can take place within a short period.

This kind of learning is not new. When children play with dolls, cars, building bricks, and other toys, they are learning to deal with real situations such as social interactions, coping with traffic, or recognizing geometric shapes. The toys are a representation of reality mirrored in a smaller and safer world. By experimenting in this world, children learn principles, patterns and ways of behaving which go beyond playing with toys and which can be used in the real world. Very young children learn the workings of systems such as language, without being taught: they experiment, observe, draw conclusions and adjust their behaviour accordingly (Senge, 1990a: 313).

Learning by means of objects such as toys is not confined to children. Members of organizations and managers also use microworlds in order to learn (Senge, 1990a). Exercises such as role-playing, team-building and project organization are used to improve teamwork. Unfortunately, however, the range of exercises available to members of organizations is fairly limited, since most tasks focus on one aspect only and do not take account of the whole pattern of relationships present in the system. Role-playing games, for example, concentrate on interpersonal communication skills, but they cannot reflect the full complexity of human interactions within the organization.

However, thanks to the development of computer applications, it is now possible to simulate complex management interactions within a company. The simulations permit the user to reflect on mental models, to test them and to modify them as needed. Microworlds of this kind are useful in developing and testing strategies and courses of action, and in creating visions and rules. 'Gradually, they are becoming a new type of "practice field" for management teams, places where teams will learn how to learn together while engaging their most important business issues' (Senge, 1990a: 315).

According to de Geus (1988), organizational learning occurs in three ways: through teaching, through changing the rules of the game and through experimenting (or play). Play is probably the least used and at the same time the most powerful aid to learning (Senge, 1990a). Its advantage is that it provides an opportunity to study complex situations, develop strategies and analyze results without running the risk of failure and having to pay the price.

Example: Business games

Business games are based on the principle of learning by doing. The procedure is to look at actual problems and develop strategies which might be expected to work in reality. Individuals or groups have to select from a range of options those which seem, from various points of view, to be the most rational. The game does not end with selecting the options: for each decision, an operational plan must be produced for putting the option into practice within the organization. Today's business games may be compared to the general staff of an army, which evaluates various situations in a war and develops possible strategies and plans of action. In a business situation, managers commit serious mistakes by following a trial-and-error procedure; today, people can 'learn by doing' in a microworld, thus minimizing the risk of failure. Technical progress in computing has made it possible to simulate the functioning of companies in a realistic manner. Many software programs are available for simulating various aspects of the business environment, for example the state of the market, the competition, and so forth. This serves as a basis for finding solutions to problems. De Geus (1988) compares computer simulation programs to a pilot's flight simulator since managers are able to test themselves in extreme situations and discover alternative courses of action. Discovering these different options is a first step towards learning since individual frames of reference are tested and interaction between individuals leads to new collective insights.

Case study 9 ⎯⎯⎯⎯⎯⎯⎯⎯⎯⎯⎯⎯

Tanaland

This study shows how simulation games can help people to develop a feel for handling complexity. These games help trainees or managers to grasp complexity, recognize mistakes in thinking about complex situations, and to improve strategic management decisions and interventions in a system.

Tanaland is a computer simulation of an area in East Africa (Figure 32) (Dörner, 1989: 22). Through the middle of Tanaland flows the Owanga river, which broadens to form Lake Mukwa. On Lake Mukwa stands the town of Lamu, surrounded by fruit plantations, gardens and an area of woodland. Lamu and the surrounding area are inhabited by the Tupi, a tribe which lives by farming and gardening. In the north and south of the country are steppes. In the north, around the small town of Kiwa, live the Moros. The Moros are a nomadic tribe who keep cattle and sheep.

During the computer simulation, subjects are given the task of caring for the well-being of the inhabitants of Tanaland and of the whole region. These subjects have full power to intervene in any way they like; there are no constraints. They can order hunts, for example, or fertilize fields or set up irrigation systems. The subjects have a total of six opportunities to collect information, plan measures and make decisions. These measures determine the fate of Tanaland for the next ten years. In each new phase of intervention, the subjects are able to review their results, i.e. their successes and failures, and to reverse or modify their decisions.

In most cases, there is an initial growth in the population, because

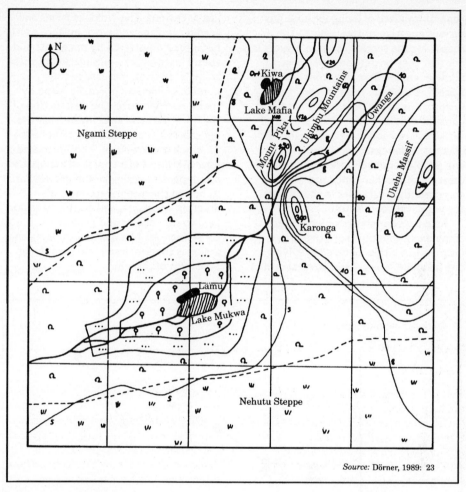

Figure 32 Tanaland.

measures were taken which at first improved the food supply and medical services. This gives the players the feeling that the problems have been solved. However, they have unwittingly installed a hidden time-bomb, which only explodes after a period of years, and which results in general starvation. Most subjects find that after about the eighty-eighth month, they have created an uncontrollable and catastrophic food shortage because modern developments have made the population dependent on food and medical supplies. The problems which were urgent at the outset, for example health care, have clearly been solved without regard for the new problems which were being created. The situation becomes catastrophic: while the rate of growth of the food supply levelled off, the population increased exponentially.

However, some players do stabilize the population and thus raise the general standard of living without any serious negative consequences. The reason for the success of these players is not that they possess any specialist knowledge, but that they consider the system as a whole. In a network-type system, it is rarely possible to consider one aspect in isolation; usually, several variables are controlled together. If side-effects are disregarded, the solving of one problem can easily result in the creation of another, since the corresponding variables in the system are negatively correlated.

Attempts to solve problems in a complex system can therefore prove ultimately fruitless because in solving one problem, one creates several others

just as serious. The yields of farms and gardens in Tanaland were meagre partly because of infestation by mice, rats and apes. However, the elimination of these animals led to an increase in the numbers of insects normally eaten by them. Furthermore, the destruction of the mice, rats and apes meant that the big cats lost their usual prey and began to attack the livestock. This illustrates how the result of a course of action does not depend on a single element within it, but on the interrelatedness of different elements, and on the attention paid to side-effects and remote consequences. Networked thinking and action is therefore suitable for solving problems of this kind.

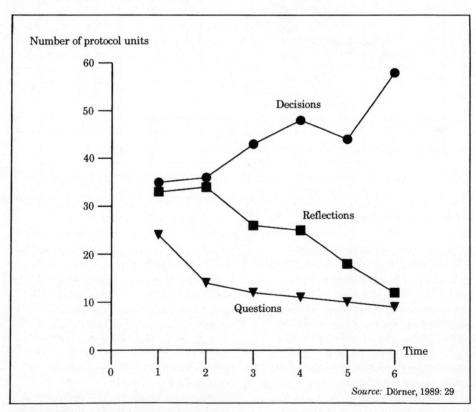

Source: Dörner, 1989: 29

Figure 33 Decisions, reflections and questions.

An analysis was made of the amount of time that subjects devote to 'decision-making', 'reflecting upon the general situation and possible solutions', and 'asking questions'. It emerged that at the beginning of the exercise, the subjects spent most of their time in reflection and asking questions, but as the exercise progressed, decision-making became the major activity (Figure 33).

The subjects believe that they have at their disposal the means which they need to solve Tanaland's problems. They build up for themselves a picture of the structure of Tanaland and act accordingly, without paying sufficient attention to possible alternative courses (Dörner, 1987).

This experiment shows how thoughts, emotions, moods and value systems interact when people have to decide what to do. The following clear parallels with real situations emerge:

■ Acting without stopping to analyze the situation
■ Ignoring side-effects and the more remote consequences
■ Ignoring the ways in which processes develop
■ Methodism: believing that one has the right methods because no negative effects have appeared
■ Escape into planning projects; cynical reactions to failure

This example shows how a simulation game can simulate reality, and how individuals and groups can learn from the ways in which situations develop. Learning takes place through the feedback on performance which is given after the game. Trial and error which would be risky in business decisions can be carried out first in a game.

Case study 10

Use of a microworld in a company planning seminar

Senge (1990a) describes how the microworld technique was used by a top management team at a two-day planning seminar. Four months previously, this team had agreed to reach a sales target of US$2 billion in four years. The members of the team had supported this goal and were committed to it. However, the vice-president of sales was uncomfortable. At the same time, he did not want his colleagues to think that he lacked commitment to the goal. His main concern was not to be seen as a 'nay sayer', especially since he had a reputation as an effective problem-solver.

The top management team went into a two-day planning retreat to examine the consequences of the sales plan, using the microworld technique to simulate the future state of the business. They soon realized that the plan was based on assumptions of which the team had not previously been aware. The plan had been to achieve 20 per cent yearly growth in sales by increasing the sales personnel by 20 per cent. The underlying assumption here was that the productivity of sales personnel would remain constant over the years: 20 per cent more sales personnel, 20 per cent more output. The next question was, how to recruit 20 per cent more salespeople with the same abilities as those already employed, so that the plan could be fulfilled. This led to a discussion of the differences between experienced and inexperienced sales staff, the training that would have to be given to the new recruits, and the possibility of luring employees away from competitors. The team then realized that the initial figure of US$2 billion would have to be revised. This was confirmed when the assumptions were built into four-year computer models and the sales figures calculated. The different teams made vain efforts to develop a strategy which would take them at least somewhere near the US$2 billion figure. They found that in the fourth year alone, the sales team would have to be doubled in order to achieve a balance between experienced and inexperienced members. This would mean an explosion in personnel costs. Enough salespeople could have been recruited to reach the US$2 billion projection, but the computer simulation showed that the inexperienced salespeople would constitute an increasing proportion of the team, which would lead to falling average productivity. When the president asked whether the senior management team still wanted to stick to the four-year plan, nobody answered. Some additional critical factors were discussed, and it became increasingly clear that the plan could not be fulfilled (Senge, 1990a).

The computer-simulated microworld provided the management team with a realistic picture of the future. Through working together to construct a collective view of reality, the group members learned to question their assumptions. They saw that they could either change the goal or restructure their sales organization. The microworld experience had forced the managers to be confronted with the

interdependencies of the system, and clarified the consequences of their plans: 'some of the most interesting learnings that come out of microworlds come from discovering implications for the future, when decisions play out in what had been unrecognized organizational systems' (Senge, 1990a: 320).

Senge lists the following as key issues which are being studied in relation to the use of microworlds to accelerate organizational learning:

1. Comparing the microworld and the real world
   ■ Revealing hidden assumptions
   ■ Discovering their inconsistency and incompleteness
2. Speeding up and slowing down time
   ■ Revealing short-term and long-term effects
3. Compressing space
   ■ Becoming aware of consequences which will arise in distant parts of the organization
4. Isolation of variables
   ■ Control of individual variables
5. Experimental orientation
   ■ Trying out new actions and procedures without having to take the consequences
6. Pauses for reflection
   ■ The chance to question actions
7. Theory-based strategy
   ■ Use of models to reveal the complexity of the organization
8. Institutional memory
   ■ Storage of knowledge and experience

These qualities of microworlds make them useful for facilitating learning. Using teamwork in microworlds is essential for creating a shared picture of reality and revealing existing norms and values. 'Future microworlds for teams will allow managers to play out their real-world roles and understand more deeply how those roles interact' (Senge, 1990a: 337). When teams use microworlds effectively to think about the future, organizational learning can be facilitated.

3 Scenario technique

Scenarios offer a framework for thought: possible developments within the organization can be modelled, and potential for change can be revealed. In order to plan useful interventions, we need to be able to visualize future developments in their entirety (Figure 34). Situations change daily as a result of their internal

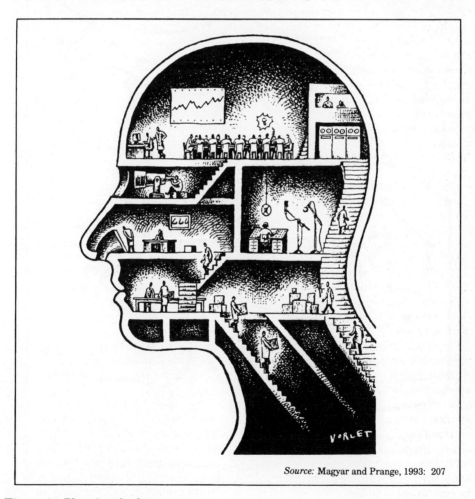

Source: Magyar and Prange, 1993: 207

Figure 34 Planning the future

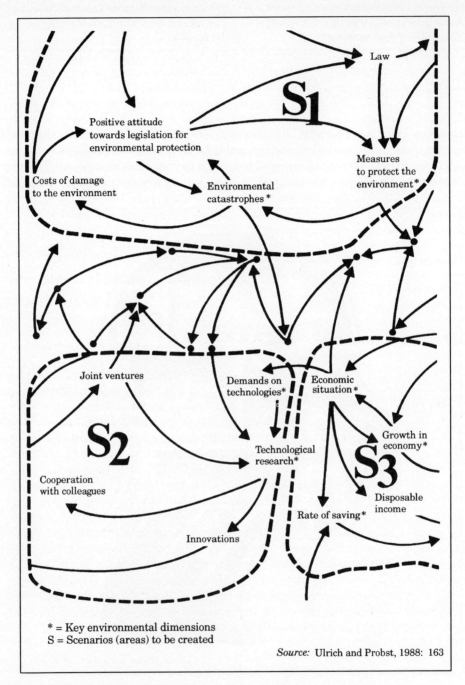

Law

S₁

Positive attitude
towards legislation for
environmental protection

Costs of damage
to the environment

Environmental
catastrophes *

Measures
to protect the
environment*

Joint ventures

Demands on
technologies*

Economic
situation *

S₂

Growth in
economy*

S₃

Cooperation
with colleagues

Technological
research*

Disposable
income

Rate of saving*

Innovations

* = Key environmental dimensions
S = Scenarios (areas) to be created

Source: Ulrich and Probst, 1988: 163

Figure 35 Determining different parts of the scenario.

dynamics, and they cannot necessarily be understood or predicted from the outside. A problem-solver who wishes to raise an organization's capacity for action will be successful if he can find measures appropriate to the future situation. From the planning point of view, today's state of affairs is simply a point of departure. Anticipation of future developments is more important. Thinking about the future is essential in choosing a course of action which will permit opportunities to be exploited, and future dangers to be foreseen (Ulrich and Probst, 1988). The vital step is to consider the future and to recognize in what respects tomorrow will be different from today.

The purpose of the scenario technique is for members of the organization to work together to form expectations about future changes. Forecasts cannot be made with certainty, because the outcomes of dynamic interdependent processes and complex situations cannot be foreseen. However, possible developments can be considered and used as a basis for making justifiable decisions. It is true that we cannot predict the future; still, we need not give up when faced by complex and dynamic problems. A system cannot change arbitrarily; it varies within certain limits which determine its behavioural space and which can be described. The scenario technique is a method for considering possible changes within a given behavioural space.

Example: Strategic environment scenarios

Describing scenarios means considering possible future situations of a complex system, basing that consideration on certain assumptions. Present information determines the assumptions, so a degree of uncertainty attaches to them. Since the situation may not develop within the assumed behavioural limits of the system, and strategies will therefore be inappropriate, it is advisable to develop several scenarios, each with strategies for dealing with a variety of situations. The activity also helps one to gain a better feel for the potential behaviours of systems, and thus acts as a trigger for learning processes. As a rule, scenarios are developed separately for different areas, then integrated to form an overall pattern (Figure 35).

Scenarios give members of the organization an opportunity, in group workshops, to discuss different views of the company. Working together to develop the scenarios becomes a learning process because assumptions are questioned and goals are developed as a basis for action. Possible future circumstances are considered and measures are devised for dealing with them; this increases the organization's capacity for action since it is now equipped to deal with a range of problems which might arise at any time.

Case study 11 ─────────────────────────────

Kuoni Travel Group

Kuoni is one of the largest travel companies in Switzerland. It employs 1,400 people and deals mainly in holiday travel, though it also offers some business travel and special-interest trips. In 1991, in response to the business environment, Kuoni decided that it could best pursue appropriate strategies by restructuring and forming a group of companies. To deal with these changes, and to enable Kuoni Switzerland to react to the changing environment, network thinking was adopted.

Integrated network thinking is a way of gathering information about the world as a basis for making strategic interventions. A comprehensive view of the company is developed in order to gain some control over the future. The first step towards this is to perceive the many connections and interactions within the system. When Kuoni was planning its new business travel service, the first step was to see the interrelationships within the company, and to understand the dynamics, before making strategic decisions about the new area. Interconnections between circular causal relationships were recognized, and on this basis, possible future developments and related strategies were considered (Fankhauser and Probst, 1993).

The first step in Kuoni's strategic planning was to set goals from various points of view, define the problem and construct a model of it. A small group then produced a network diagram showing the interrelationships between goals and influential factors (Figure 36). The result was a condensed description of a situation viewed from various angles, so as to yield an integrated picture of the organization. Time factors and the relative strengths of different

influences were included. The network diagram became a dynamic model which could then be used for simulation purposes.

A dynamic view of the current situation is, however, not a sufficient basis for planning; we also need to know how the situation might develop in the future. Anticipation of possible future changes is a vital element. With this in mind, Kuoni considered several variants of the future and examined environmental configurations which seemed probable. The scenario technique was used as a way of visualizing future situations and their implications, and thinking through possible courses of action. In practice, a basic scenario was developed which, using the information then available, seemed the most likely pattern of development. However, other possibilities were also considered, leading to alternative scenarios of varying degrees of optimism. These scenarios, each of which was judged to be either favourable or unfavourable to the company, formed the basis of reserve strategies which could be used to tackle unexpected developments or mishaps. This enriched the organization's capacity for action and knowledge, and thus initiated organizational learning. From the point of view of learning, the teamwork involved in developing the network diagram, the analysis of relationships, and the 'play' with scenarios in workshops were particularly fruitful.

The network served Kuoni as a basis for developing scenarios for different areas of the business environment. It formed a background against which scenarios, optimistic or pessimistic views, or specific questions could be

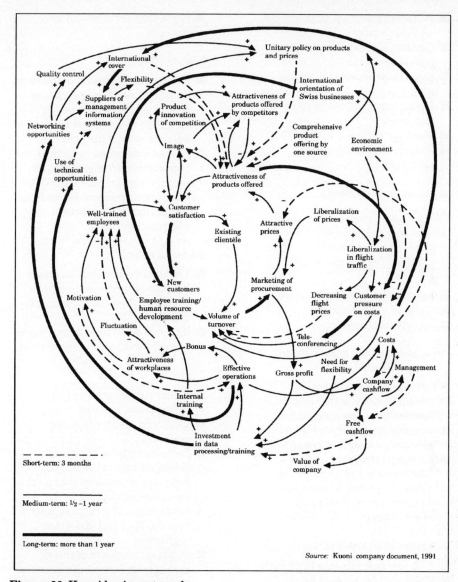

Quality control

International
cover

Flexibility

Unitary policy on products
and prices

Suppliers of
management
information
systems

International
orientation of
Swiss businesses

Networking
opportunities

Product
innovation
of competition

Attractiveness of
products offered
by competitors

Comprehensive
product
offering by
one source

Economic
environment

Use of
technical
opportunities

Image

Attractiveness of
products offered

Well-trained
employees

Customer
satisfaction

Attractive
prices

Liberalization
of prices

Existing
clientèle

Liberalization
in flight
traffic

Motivation

New
customers

Marketing of
procurement

Decreasing
flight
prices

Customer
pressure
on costs

Employee training/
human resource
development

Volume of
turnover

Fluctuation

Tele-
conferencing

Costs

Bonus

Attractiveness
of workplaces

Effective
operations

Gross profit

Need for
flexibility

Management

Company
cashflow

Internal
training

Free
cashflow

Investment
in data
processing/training

Value of
company

Short-term: 3 months

Medium-term: ½ –1 year

Long-term: more than 1 year

Source: Kuoni company document, 1991

Figure 36 Kuoni business travel.

discussed (for example, crisis scenario for the Gulf War). A scenario of this kind was used by various management committees to consider the consequences of entry to the EEA or EC. The following extract gives an idea of its form and content.

Scenario for entry to EEA/EC (August 1991)

Assumptions

■ Far-reaching EEA treaty, coming close to EC entry

- EC internal market does not cut off Switzerland
- German unification stimulates positive growth
- Long-term growth in Eastern Bloc
- Swiss capital continues to be expensive
- Shortage of capital in the 1990s
- Process of concentration continues

Business developments

Effects of total European integration include those due to larger market and those due to more intensive competition. There are three main consequences:

- International division of work
- Increase in productivity
- Structural change

These could proceed in parallel, and influence each other:

- *International work-sharing*: production in the cheapest place, Switzerland loses importance
- *Increase in productivity*: more efficient production, lower prices
- *Structural changes*: differentiation of products into strategic groups, concentration, formation of strategic alliances and coalitions

Integration after 10 years:

- 4 – 6 per cent increase in growth
- 8 per cent decrease in prices

Travel market

General economic developments affect travel market in two ways:

- Short- to medium-term effects on branch structure of industry and supply

- More long-term effects on demand

Supply effects

- Concentration leads to pressure on prices, and foreign suppliers appear on the Swiss market
- Language and cultural solidarity become self-limiting factors
- Pressure develops to form cooperative arrangements to support volume business. Quality improvements must be made as protection against foreign competition

Demand effects

- The volume of travel increases because of increased prosperity and more financial resources for travel
- Internationalization brings higher mobility and leads to more travel

Summary of effects

- General pressure on prices, falling profit margins
- Language as extra limiting criterion
- Pressure to form cooperative arrangements in the buying, production and sales area on the European market
- Penetration of foreign suppliers into the low- and mid-price segments
- Increase in volume of travel throughout Europe as a result of long-term increases in prosperity
- Complete liberalization of air travel
- Tariff chaos

When the scenarios were developed and their implications described, the group moved on to look at opportunities and threats. This process

Scenarios	Economic and political developments	Threats	Opportunities
Basic scenario Deregulation (extract)	• Freeing of flight tariffs	• Widespread tariff chaos	• Market advantage can be gained by installing newest technology (robot software)
			• Volume-dependent cost prices become more important, concentration of volume in European market
	• Collapse of prices in European air travel	• Lower prices do not lead to greater volume of passengers as expected	• Increase in need for management information in the travel area, especially at international level
		• Turnover-dependent sales commissions fall	
	• Aging of fleet because of lack of investment	• Air travel becomes unsafe because of technical troubles	• Rail travel becomes a real alternative within a 600 km radius
Alternative scenario 1 (entirely deregulated market)	• Total collapse of prices to all destinations	• Marked and sudden drop in prices combined with takeovers and collapse of prominent air companies	• New negotations on margins
	•	•	•
	•	•	•
	•	•	•
Alternative scenario 2, or crisis scenario	• Escalation in state crisis	•Travel market becomes uncertain; reticence and reorientation of behaviour	• New technologies, new markets
	• Reduction in oil supplies	•Prices take the full impact of increases in oil prices	• Advice on cost management
			•
	• Gross national product sinks	•Negative growth forecasts and higher fares	•
			•
			Source: Kuoni company document, 1991

Figure 37 Kuoni business travel: opportunities and threats.

is shown in Figure 37.

Thinking through and interpreting the scenarios is a creative process which requires more than just a methodical approach. It means gathering and evaluating a variety of information from different sources, combining them with one's own ideas, and applying them to the problem, so that the essentials can be identified and patterns of behaviour recognized. This process of combining existing knowledge and developing new insights is an essential process leading to organizational learning.

Case study 12

Royal Dutch Petroleum/Shell

The Royal Dutch Petroleum/Shell group is an international oil company with 82,000 employees. For the second largest company in Europe, strategic planning has been an important contribution to learning. The director of planning, strategy and organization for Shell Germany writes that continuous group learning processes and the business measures which result from them are necessary conditions of success (Hoffman, 1993). Most decision-making processes within the company are really learning processes: the participants start with differing opinions, attitudes and values, their differences are revealed during discussion, and a new picture develops. Decisions made as a result of group processes have proved to be of high quality, and more valuable than unreflected decisions taken by individuals. The Shell Groups make use of scenarios as thought models for accelerating group decision-making processes.

Scenarios may be regarded as the fundamental instrument of learning because they offer a means of changing mental models as well as of aligning them. When participants analyze a business area of the company which is the setting for their actions, they achieve greater clarity with regard to their experiences, attitudes and values.

The use of scenarios helps participants to guard against persistent thought habits or believing that things will be the same in ten years' time. They compel individuals and groups to confront economic and social trends, and help them to recognize principles and interactions in a complex world. This can lead to changes in mental models and thereby initiate organizational learning. Different members of an organization can only harmonize their cognitive maps if they work together to confirm or reject the assumptions implicit in the scenarios, and to reveal opportunities and risks which had not previously been taken into account.

In their work with scenarios, the main question for Shell is: what shall we do if something happens? Scenarios encourage the perception and processing of early warning signals. The aims are timely recognition of possible future developments such as structural changes, and to pick up weak signals.

In the Shell group, the learning process begins with the identification of issues which are important to the company. To this end, the planning department carries out a survey of employees. To obtain a comprehensive picture, internal members of the organization collaborate in developing scenarios with outsiders who are experts in relevant fields. After the scenario group has held workshops to develop two 'raw scenarios', these scenarios are discussed with the appropriate people in the company who focus on regions. The planning group then puts together a global scenario which serves as a basis for organizational decision-making processes.

For each scenario or issue, the implications of possible developments are sketched out and important economic data are recorded so that appropriate measures can be taken. In all the companies within the Shell group, the central planning department offers special workshops so that even if the different business units are not involved in the development of the scenarios, they are nevertheless kept informed of future challenges.

The Shell Group of companies clearly attaches considerable importance to internal learning processes. Many employees take part in building scenarios, and thus in constructing mental models of the future. As people interact to adjust and harmonize their mental models, a shared frame of reference emerges.

4 Strategic control

Strategic control is the periodic checking of the premises on which strategic planning is based, the recording of progress in implementing strategies and the introduction of corrective measures as appropriate. The outcomes of human actions are not predictable, but simulation techniques can help to evaluate their likely results, and thus to retain some measure of control. Discrepancies between actual and predicted outcomes suggest that corrections need to be made: guidelines, rules and goals may need adjustments.

Strategy control also includes the task of revealing areas where development of new strategies is possible or necessary. Controlling may lead to the development of new business areas.

In complex and dynamic situations it is not always easy, or even possible, to assess the effects of various actions. There is a need for an integrated tool for strategic control. By analyzing the management cycle in a company, solutions may be found which will enable managers to take the proper measures. Early-warning indicators permit managers to deal with changes or deviations in time, i.e. to act rather than react. It is important to give feedback promptly, at the right place and in a suitable form (Probst and Gomez, 1991; Ulrich and Probst, 1988) (Figure 38).

Example: Measurement systems ————————————————————

Measurement systems are used for checking processes. The output is compared to the input and the resulting information leads to actions, policies, behaviours

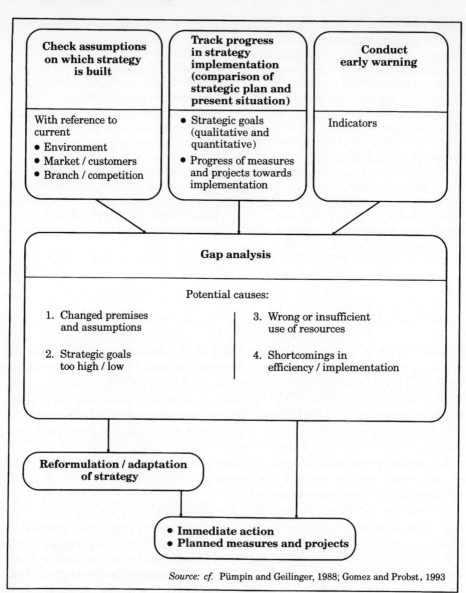

Figure 38 Strategic control.

or goals. Where strategic processes are implemented, for example where a new policy is being introduced and its effects monitored, measurement systems provide an instrument of evaluation and correction. Agreed measures are evaluated in order to identify improvements, make plans for the future and assess the need for further checks and corrections. A good measurement system is one in which the important early warning signs are monitored and correct use is made of the information obtained.

Case study 13

Skandia AFS

Skandia is a Scandinavian financial services company. In 1994, the group had a gross income of SK 54 billion. In 1994, one of its largest and fastest-growing divisions, Skandia Assurance and Financial Services (or AFS), achieved a gross income of SK 25 billion. The division recognized the importance of its knowledge capital, and decided to carry out an assessment of intellectual assets. The company believed that its future success depended upon its ability to recognize and use the knowledge that it possessed.

Skandia believed that intellectual capital is the only real asset apart from the traditional balance sheet. The company regarded learning, and the evaluation of the outcomes of learning, as the only real source of competitive advantage in the future. Developing a measurement system of learning outcomes therefore became a primary objective. To achieve this objective, Skandia AFS set itself the following mission, as described in its annual report:

> Operations within AFS should feature an accelerated, steeper learning curve that will rapidly integrate corporate knowledge into tangible assets and enable AFS to apply it with maximum competitive effect — turning AFS into both a learning and teaching organization.

The programme consisted of the following four steps:

- Identify intangible and soft assets and make them more visible and measurable
- Use blueprinting and prototyping to package knowledge and make it reusable
- Cultivate and channel intellectual assets by means of training and development of knowledge workers and use of information technology
- Increase the leverage and value of knowledge by speeding up its re-use and through skills and application transfer

Fundamental to this programme was the development of a measurement system for the purpose of assessing the division's intellectual capital. Traditional instruments such as balance sheets cannot show the organization's soft assets. Skandia therefore developed its own system for evaluating soft assets.

The first step in the measurement of the company's intellectual assets was to draw up lists of the various components of the human capital, customer capital and structural capital. These lists were put together in the 'Balanced Annual Report on Intellectual Capital'. Within Skandia the human capital consists of the skills of individuals; the customer capital consists of relationships with customers, and structural capital is 'all that is left behind when the staff is gone'. Skandia regards the combination of these assets as constituting its intellectual capital.

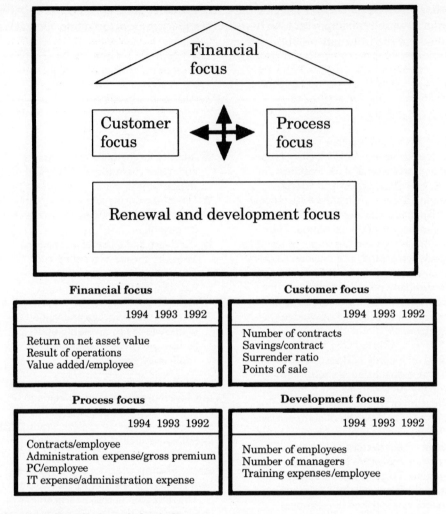

Figure 39 Skandia knowledge indicators.

Skandia set about developing a measurement system which could be used for purposes of strategic controlling. The result was the 'Skandia AFS business navigator', based on knowledge indicators (Figure 39). The company was interested in measuring changes in its intellectual assets, rather than their absolute value. It therefore chose quantitative indices of change in intellectual capital, for example turnover of new products, training costs, proportion of employees below the age of 35, number of accounts per employee. These indices were published. More importantly, they are a subject of discussion within the business unit, and they form the basis for decisions about how to make the company into a learning organization.

Skandia uses this measurement system as the first step towards the creation of a learning organization. The business navigator is a feedback system which provides information which the company needs in order to identify and record knowledge, to foster its development, and to make it useful throughout the organization. The company then increases its intellectual assets by means of employee development and training, and uses information technology to make knowledge more accessible.

9

Learning by developing
a structure

1 The structural context

Structures both permit and exclude possible courses of action. Some rules limit
our freedom of movement; others strengthen innovative and creative processes.
The purpose of the creation of an organizational structure is to provide a
framework in which events and possibilities can be ordered. Within a structural
framework, organizations may survive or develop, and they may take on various
patterns. The framework is based on formal and informal rules and measures for
shaping events. Within a structure, different organizational patterns are
determined. The reason for establishing structure is to set groundrules for
steering and supporting the company's development and ability to adapt. To
this end, the instruments and methods which the organization possesses must
be adjusted and applied appropriately.

To enable learning processes to take place within an organization, balances
must be struck between control and autonomy, order and chaos, stability and
change, and centralization and decentralization. The task of management is to
establish the right degree of structuring within a field characterized by all these
tensions. It needs to look for structural forms which will promote organizational learning and afford space for innovation and creativity. There should be
opportunities to reflect on work processes, tackle problems, recognize
opportunities and carry tasks through to completion and allow for employee

Project organization	Who: Groups Aim: Learning through problem-solving
Network structures	Who: Groups and system Aim: Learning through linkages
Cooperative arrangements	Who: System Aim: Learning through increasing problem-so

Figure 40 Development of structure as a learning process.

participation in decision-making. These criteria steer the choice of organizational forms towards temporary network structures and flat hierarchies. They suggest less division of tasks; integration of thinking, action and planning; implementation and monitoring by the same people (Sattelberger, 1991c; Probst, 1993). In general terms, there is a need for structures which will facilitate creativity, reflection, and freedom.

It is not our aim here to give detailed descriptions of the possible range of structures. We shall confine ourselves to giving a few examples of the learning involved in the process of developing structures. Organizational aids such as team organization and networks provide a basic framework for stability, creativity, flexibility, integration, etc. However, managing structural change also calls for adequate aids, procedures and processes; these include project organization, communication processes, creativity methods, aids to implementation and unfreezing methods. We concentrate here on structural processes and procedures in order to show the connection with organizational learning (Figure 40).

2 Projects as a form of organization

If a company is to function and to provide security, it must have a relatively stable form of organization. At the same time, it needs specific and temporary structures to allow it to cope with the dynamic nature of its internal and external environments, and to permit learning to take place. Projects are a form which can be superimposed on the 'permanent' structure, and which aim to create new and changing patterns of relationships between members of the organization. The combination of the two kinds of structure yields a matrix containing both temporary and permanent forms of organization: an organization within the organization. Both the relationships and the interactions amongst employees increase in density. New kinds of secondary or parallel structures continue to appear as the business world becomes ever more complex, i.e. more diverse, dynamic and discrete (Figure 41).

Traditional organization	Parallel organization
■ Routine operations – low uncertainty ■ Output as primary goal ■ Limited 'opportunities' for employees ■ Fixed job descriptions ■ Training before starting the job ■ Lengthy official channels ■ Top-down goal-setting ■ Incentives: pay, allowances (bonuses) ■ Functional specialization ■ Leadership based on position in hierarchy (authority of office)	■ Problem-solving – high uncertainty ■ Organization as primary goal ■ Substantial 'opportunities' (e.g. to participate in a taskforce) ■ Flexible job rotation ■ Training on the job ■ Short official channels ■ Bottom-up goal-setting ■ Incentives: learning opportunities, new social contacts, recognition ■ Diagonal links ■ Leadership based on expertise (personal authority)
Source: Kasper, 1990: 29 (adapted from Kanter, 1983)	

Figure 41 Parallel organization.

These parallel forms increasingly involve small, flexible teams in which power changes hands, hierarchies are fluid, and the ability to deal with risks and conflict is increased. Project teams do not have a long life: like clans (Ouchi, 1981), or clusters (Quinn-Mills, 1993), they can be arranged and rearranged. There are no long-term job descriptions, and powers of leadership and decision-making are often temporary. This makes enormous demands on team members' flexibility, competence and tolerance of pressure. It tests their skills in the areas of organization, time-management, integration, conflict mastery, etc. (Probst, 1993; Quinn-Mills, 1993).

Example: Project management

In order for project management to lead to learning it must be supported by both methods and structures (Figure 42). Both the people working on the project and others who will be affected by it must be suitably prepared; this is a requirement which is both difficult to meet and at the same time more important for the creation of a learning environment. Members of project teams must be prepared and trained for difficult tasks. Most importantly, they must develop an understanding of project work; learn how to cope with diversity; learn tolerance and social competence; improve their leadership and communication skills; and learn how to apply suitable methods and instruments when setting goals, managing finances and leading discussions (evaluation, cost control, feedback, etc.) Training should be provided not only for the 'specialists' in a prospective project team but also for as many as possible of those who will be affected by the project. Ideally, project management skills will develop in practice, with the support of experienced internal and external advisers. This makes for a wider field of learning and greater ease of implementation. However, certain inputs are needed to support organizational learning and take the process as far as it

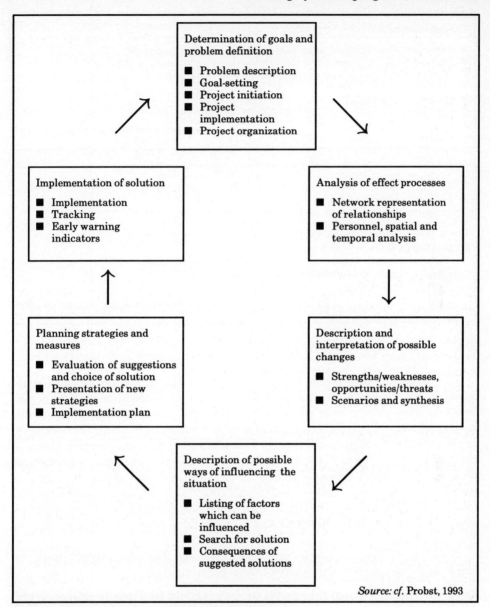

Figure 42 Aid to project management methods.

can go. These inputs are support and supervision, sharing of experience, feedback and conscious development of skills. Swissair, for example, has a longstanding policy of involving as many employees as possible in the process and giving them direct control of projects (see Figure 43 on the 1987/89 project, which involved the whole organization).

Project guidelines

■ Implementation of project under own direction (project management)
■ Optimal use of own capacities (project work according to 'militia system')
■ Creation of optimal synergy effects (working in network teams)
■ 'Structure follows function'
■ 'People follow structure'
■ Use of external advisers for technical support (not as 'chief ideologists' or 'chief designers')

Source: Swissair company documents, 1989

Reasons for projects

■ Motivation and identification
   Receptiveness to new ideas, methods and solutions
■ Acceptance and completion
   Personal commitment to realization
■ Building up skills
   Analysis of complex problems
   Thinking in strategic dimensions
   Management of change

Source: Swissair company documents, 1989

Figure 43 Swissair company documents, 1989.

The initiation of projects is one of the most important forms of internal mobilization. 'A project is a collective effort directed towards specific goals'. Projects give rise to new patterns of collective interaction and new links between people. Projects act as catalysts. According to Etzioni, there are two reasons for this: (1) projects remove constraints on persons who are lower in the hierarchy, and lead to the realization that these constraints are a senseless barrier; (2) the development of a collective awareness can lead to the removal of barriers and pressures which individually are both intangible and powerful (Naujoks, 1993). This clears the way for the development of a unique dynamic system within which the abilities and energies of members of the organization can be mobilized.

Working in project teams promotes learning, but the project must be consciously structured, and it must follow certain rules:

■ **Spreading the word**: Successful projects should be given prominence and made known throughout the firm. Success stories create a good atmosphere, and the telling of them promotes sharing of experience.

■ **Training**: Project management skills cannot be taken for granted. Training must be provided.

■ **Fostering junior talent**: Young employees should be brought into a project team as early as possible, and given commensurate responsibility.

■ **Remuneration**: Project and team skills should be recognized and should

contribute to individual performance ratings.
■ **Selection**: New employees should be selected partly for project management skills.

When these different aspects are fulfilled, the likelihood that projects will foster learning is increased.

Case study 14

Winterthur Insurances

Winterthur Insurances carried out an analysis of its structure during a period when the business climate was good, i.e. there was no immediate threat. The analysis involved the Swiss non-life insurance branch of the company. This branch employs over 500 people in head office, about 1,600 in the regional organizations, and 2,500 in the general agencies. The general policy of Winterthur is to be as close as possible to the customer: sales, management and claims are therefore decentralized as far as possible. Current success notwithstanding, it was recognized that the business environment was changing at breakneck speed, and would continue to change. This brought the flexibility and learning capacity of the organization into question. It seemed a good idea to look at issues such as the increasing competition, deregulation, excess capacity, internationalization, new sales avenues, the development of a buyers' market, pressures on costs, and cost management. A 'reorganization project' was set up to tackle these issues. From the beginning, project teams were assembled throughout the whole company. The teams held workshops to discuss the market, and the future structure of the organization.

The project progressed through several phases (see Figure 44). As a first step, a large team was created to formulate the problems. Defining the problem consisted essentially in identifying internal difficulties and analyzing external problem areas. An additional question was whether reorganization would provide a suitable solution for the problems under review. Goals were then set, and priorities and time limits were assigned to them. Particular attention was paid to possible side-effects, compatibility with company policy, and communication.

Following this first phase of project management, tasks were set for internal and external project workers, with various instructions relating to structure and process. The essential elements in this 'ideal' project plan were:

■ Defining the problem
■ Setting the goals of the project
■ Identifying project leaders
■ Assigning team members
■ Setting team tasks
■ Clarifying authority to make decisions
■ Assigning responsibility
■ Defining the structural form
■ Identifying areas where the company would be affected
■ Identifying obstacles and limitations
■ Setting the schedule
■ Agreeing on the budget
■ Establishing communication links

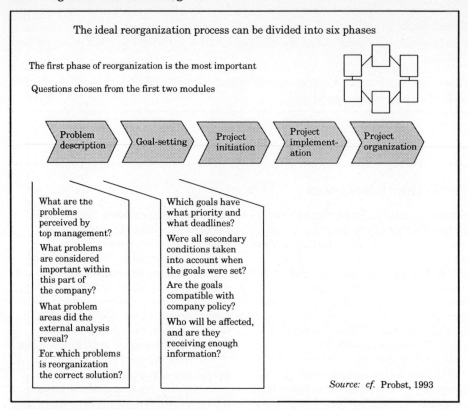

The ideal reorganization process can be divided into six phases

The first phase of reorganization is the most important

Questions chosen from the first two modules

Problem description | Goal-setting | Project initiation | Project implement-ation | Project organization

What are the problems perceived by top management?

What problems are considered important within this part of the company?

What problem areas did the external analysis reveal?

For which problems is reorganization the correct solution?

Which goals have what priority and what deadlines?

Were all secondary conditions taken into account when the goals were set?

Are the goals compatible with company policy?

Who will be affected, and are they receiving enough information?

Source: cf. Probst, 1993

Figure 44 Winterthur Insurances: phases of the reorganization project.

The answers to the main questions under each of these headings were useful in the further organization of the project. Outside workers and process advisers structured the organizational process and acted as moderators and mediators. Internal employees, deliberately chosen from different departments, were given functions within the project team and were assigned tasks, responsibilities and areas of authority.

At the beginning of the project, the concept of the workshop and the role of the project team advisers were discussed and formalized. Interestingly, the ways in which members had understood the project up to this point were now reviewed and corrected.

A company's readiness and ability to learn depend to a large extent on its insight into the reasons why project work and reorganization are necessary. The dynamics of change were studied during the first workshop, which was devoted to an analysis of various factors in the internal and external environments: technology, strategy, company culture, power structures, company structure and environment. This clarified the need for reorganization and helped the team to look at the current structure of the company in the light of future environmental demands. Members worked together to identify the reasons why reorganization was necessary. A process of this kind is essential if goals

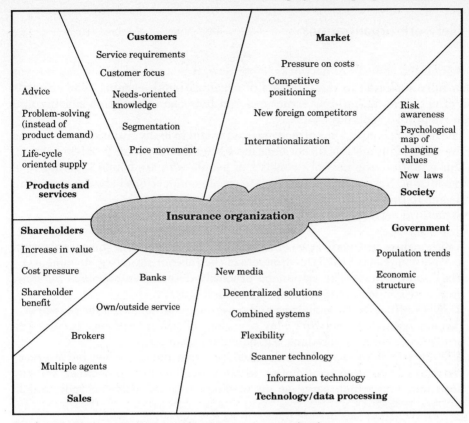

Figure 45 Goals and priorities of an insurance organization.

are to be met and the essential characteristics of the new organizational structure made clear. It was therefore important for the project team members to analyze the situation from different points of view (Figure 45) before formulating their goals.

The purpose of the workshops was to examine the structure of Winterthur Insurances, Switzerland, and, at the same time, to make the organization of the project more meaningful. The process of structural development led to learning in the company because employees from different departments were involved in team activity. This increased the density of the network of relationships and thus facilitated communication. Contacts between employees were increased, and discussion took place over a fairly long time-span. Interactions amongst members of the organization were thus strengthened, and knowledge which would be useful in the future was shared. The intention was that the project would exist in parallel with the basic organization. An essential feature of this kind of project management which promotes learning is that it stresses interactions within groups rather than focusing on instruments.

3 Network organizations

Although the concept of networks is not new, it is a notion which has not yet been fully exploited in the interests of organizational learning. The efficient use of networks in building structures can increase information-sharing and improve problem-solving skills.

The network concept has already proved useful in many situations. Networks in the sense of roundtable discussions have been used for joint problem-solving. In this situation, the network consists of people who are bound together by a common goal. Networks are also used to create connections between operating units and to link whole organizations together.

Structural networks have the following characteristics:

■ Relationships are qualitative and abstract. The members of the organization are more important than the products of the relationships (e.g. documents).
■ The limits of networks cannot be precisely defined; autonomous persons, groups or systems act independently of each other.
■ Responsibility, decision-making and power are shared across the network.
■ Persons within the network play a variety of roles; they may occupy key positions or connect positions, e.g. boundary-spanners.
■ A balance develops between individual interests and the collective interest.
■ Networks have values and norms which provide cohesion between the key positions, and which serve as an ideological 'glue' between individuals. (Harris, 1985: 254)

If networks are to be an instrument of organizational learning, participants must be open and be willing to share opinions and attitudes. Networks challenge their members to be understanding and accepting, to support creative processes and to stimulate democratic discussions so that higher-level learning can take place. The discussion process provides opportunities for analyzing the ways in which people work together, and the basic 'rules of the game' (values, norms, etc.). The analysis of communication structures are important for seeking solutions to problems. The building of interpersonal relationships within the organization increases the ability to act and the potential to solve problems. It creates and extends the knowledge base, which means that future problems can be mastered in new ways.

Increasing the knowledge base is only one of the ways in which networks can lead to organizational learning. Networks enable people to work outside their hierarchical structures and to reach decisions more quickly; they also foster an *esprit de corps*. 'A much more important aspect is the fact that in every company, interpersonal relationships are extremely significant. Examples of such relationships are "good contacts", or stable coalitions (cliques, groups of interdependent persons), which facilitate sharing of information (insider-

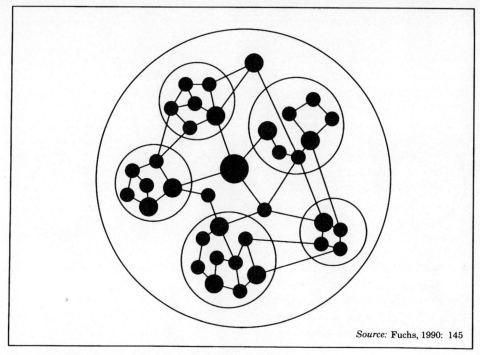

Source: Fuchs, 1990: 145

Figure 46 Networks within and between structures.

knowledge), shorten decision processes (favoured access), and provide spontaneous, non-bureaucratic support in difficult situations' (Neuberger, 1991: 232).

Networks thus facilitate organizational learning in two ways. First, network formation promotes interpersonal sharing of knowledge and increases problem-solving skills. Secondly, the formation and use of networks can focus attention on the importance of the non-personal and informal aspects of structure. An attempt is made to clarify this concept in Figure 46.

Example: Heterarchy

As current management idiom, heterarchy is often used to mean the opposite of hierarchy, although this does not necessarily do justice to the real meaning of the word (Hedlund, 1986; Türk, 1989). A heterarchy is really an organization which has a polycentric structure and which does not, therefore, function according to simple hierarchical and centralist principles. The idea of the concept is that the complexity of our society cannot be understood or mastered by individuals. However, a number of individuals may be better equipped to deal

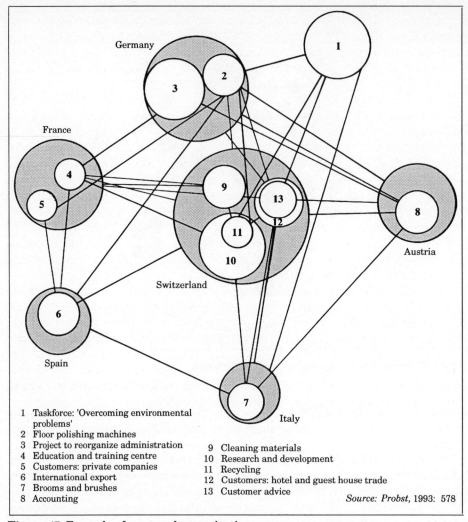

Figure 47 Example of a network organization.

with different situations. Interactions among several individuals are reflected in a heterarchy.

A heterarchy is based on fluctuating hierarchical relationships between individuals or systems. Like the relationships in hierarchies — which are based on authority, status, prestige, etc. — the relationships in a heterarchy can be reversed as necessary (Probst, 1993). Links between organizational units are often loose and their external relationships are not fixed, so coalitions of all kinds may emerge. Because of the strategic responsibilities of the subsystems, each unit must possess information about the whole. This leads to the formation of critical interdependencies between the units. Heterarchies are characterized by normative control. They must aim to use the characteristics described by Harris (see above) to build up networks which enable the whole organization to increase its capacity for action and its ability to solve problems. These are the qualities which guarantee the ability to learn.

Honda is a company which tries to operate as a heterarchy. It has never had international headquarters; decisions are made in the place where the necessary information is available. Honda seems to have succeeded in developing procedures which support the decision process in different situations. The basis of this is a shared language which is used for thinking and communicating in forty countries. A leading Honda employee has said that the company will have achieved total globalization when Honda Japan is only one of many global companies operating at the same level (Iikubo, 1990).

Figure 47 shows a polycentric organizational form, a heterarchy. The company is organized according to functions located in different countries. The network structure permits contacts and exchange of information, and thus provides a context for learning. The typical network has a changing structure, because that part which possesses the most information and knowledge 'dominates'. When a new situation arises and different questions are asked, the part which was dominant returns to its original position in the network, making room for other parts. The management structure in Honda, Schläpfer Embroideries, and Forbo International can be interpreted as heterarchies (see Case studies 2 and 15 in this book). Other examples such as cluster organizations (Quinn-Mills, 1993) or team organizations (Staehle, 1991; Lawler, 1992) follow principles similar to those of heterarchies.

Case study 15 ⎯⎯⎯⎯⎯⎯⎯⎯⎯⎯⎯⎯⎯⎯⎯

Forbo International

Forbo International is the world leader in linoleum production and specializes in floor and wall coverings. It is an international holding consisting of 100 companies. At the headquarters in Switzerland, the directors of the holding make policy decisions for the business areas (Figure 48).

In principle, the Forbo companies are networked at two levels. At the first level are the networks within individual business areas; at the second is the network which joins all the business areas together. Individual companies within the holding move in their own orbits around a centrally coordinated strategy. Each company has a core business and integrated responsibility for development, production and sales. The core business can be extended by means of alliances. The operational connections multiply the skills present in the network, and at the same time hold the whole structure together. The satellite companies also have links with the centre. These exist for the purposes

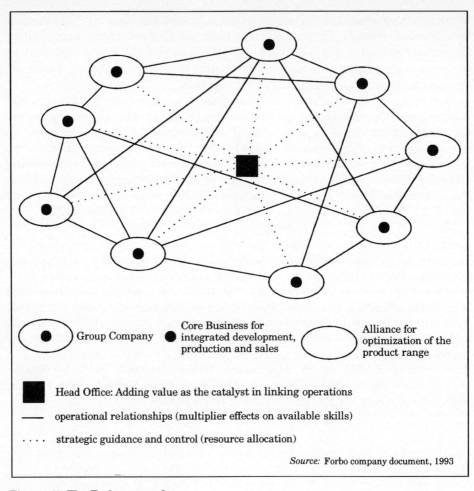

Group Company

Core Business for integrated development, production and sales

Alliance for optimization of the product range

Head Office: Adding value as the catalyst in linking operations

——— operational relationships (multiplier effects on available skills)

· · · · strategic guidance and control (resource allocation)

Source: Forbo company document, 1993

Figure 48 The Forbo network.

of strategic control and assignment of resources. If links at all levels are efficient, the speed of communication increases, as does the transfer of competence and know-how. Forbo has an interdisciplinary databank; this is an indispensable feature of an economically rational network. It shows where available resources can be put to even better use. This system may be regarded as Forbo's stock market for proficiency and available capacity. Forbo has developed a network which increases its capacity for action by linking organizational units with each other, thus enabling the units to exchange information amongst themselves. By developing these links between units and fostering greater interaction, a first step towards learning has been taken.

Case study 16 ─────────────────

McDonalds

The philosophy of McDonalds is to sell universally standardized products in self-service restaurants. Raw materials are transformed into end-products within a short time and with relatively low labour costs. The Tayloristic form of work organization permits the use of unqualified personnel, contributes to low production costs, and helps to maintain quality, speed, cleanliness and value (QSCV). McDonalds has adopted the franchise system, which means it can put this philosophy into effect around the world. In 1988 the company had 560,000 employees worldwide and achieved a turnover of about SF 22.5 billion (Sydow, 1992).

The company has suppliers in the following sectors: agriculture, food industry, packaging industry and furniture industry. The McDonalds network of companies from the above-mentioned industries is characterized by close and stable relationships between the companies. It is one of McDonalds practices to prescribe certain quality standards not only for its immediate suppliers but also for suppliers who are further back in the value chain. This chain of quality standards is guaranteed by careful choice of contract suppliers and by constant controls and inspections. Initiatives in product and process development come not only from McDonalds itself but also from its suppliers. A McDonalds employee has said that over the years, the suppliers have to some extent become extensions of internal product development (Love, 1988: 329).

In recent years, McDonalds has tried to make a drastic reduction in the number of its suppliers, while at the same time building up long-term relationships with those who remained. This meant that it was easier to ensure quality, and that a network structure could be used in the further development of the organization. A policy of forming long-term, stable relationships was adopted as part of the network philosophy (Figure 49).

The company's 'McDonaldizing' strategy has led to savings in costs and has also brought competitive advantages and created innovative momentum. The individual restaurants are regarded as part of a whole family because they are strongly linked into the worldwide network. The company guarantees observance of its philosophy by prescribing standards (QSCV) and by involving franchisees in advertising campaigns. Close networks exist between McDonalds and its suppliers, and between McDonalds and its franchise restaurants. The McDonalds network is characterized by the increasing integration of companies which are legally independent but economically dependent. This structure means that short-term, market-determined relationships between supplier and producer are sacrificed in favour of long-term cooperative relationships. The companies can work together on product and process innovations, quality control and logistical problems. The mechanisms include coordinating activities such as intraorganizational teams, interorganizational information systems, and the development of an organizational culture built on trust. These are precisely the kinds of activity which facilitate organizational learning. Working together to solve problems and coordinating activities compels the

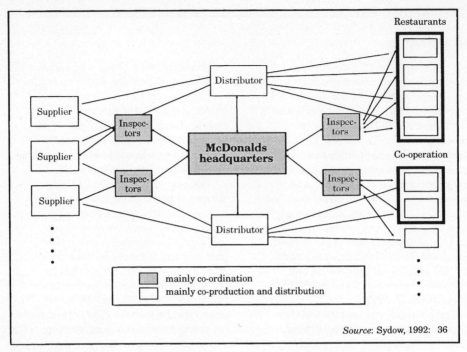

Source: Sydow, 1992: 36

Figure 49 The McDonalds network.

participants to study the opinions and objectives of the 'other' companies, and to use what they learn as a stimulus to making changes within their own organization.

4 Forms of cooperative arrangement

Cooperative arrangements are structural forms which can provide a framework for learning. Companies may enter a cooperative arrangement for strategic reasons; it offers them a way of compensating to some extent for their weaknesses, since they gain the physical resources, the markets, the know-how and the capital of the partner, thus increasing their capacity for action. There are a number of forms of cooperation which can offer these benefits. One form consists in gaining control of most of the capital of another company (acquisition); another is contractual cooperation, with or without purchase of shares; a third is an agreement to combine resources in a newly-founded firm (a joint venture). Forms of cooperation are many and varied, which makes them a flexible way of structuring an organization.

A cooperative arrangement requires coordination and integration of its constituent companies. This can make for better use of the opportunities present in the environment. When companies join together in a cooperative arrangement, new information-gathering centres, or sensors, are set up; these have a monitoring function, and they also pick up information from the environment which the partner company would otherwise be denied. Risks and opportunities are thus perceived in good time. In the case of a joint venture, the company itself may be able to exploit the opportunities detected by the sensors. A joint venture has a high degree of autonomy, which means that innovative strengths can be exploited, and new core activities and products can be tested on the market.

Attempts to use a cooperative arrangement as a way of exploiting opportunities in the environment can, it is true, lead to the realization that further resources are needed. However, these can sometimes be obtained from the partner companies. The chance to make an early response to an opportunity is in itself potential action, and gives the company an advantage and a possible avenue for development. Companies need to consider possible patterns of relationships and interdependencies which would enable them to exploit opportunities. Cooperative arrangements can help companies to increase their value; during the period of their usefulness, they can be a source of surplus value.

Different cooperative arrangements are part of a more or less complex structure of cooperative relationships. Within this system, each arrangement makes its contribution and cooperates with the others, giving rise to a network of relationships. Through these relationships, problem-solving strategies are built up which allow the parent company to increase the capacity for action. If we look at the complete range of possible structural forms, cooperative arrangements emerge as a form in which the people responsible for the various units work together in a kind of federation. They build up formal and informal networks of relationships, and are moulded in their turn by increasing autonomy. We have here the conditions needed for organizational learning. The ability to act can only be increased where people work together on problems, sharing solutions, information and technologies, and where autonomous units provide the necessary degree of freedom.

Example: Strategic alliances

Strategic alliances are cooperative arrangements between companies that share a common goal. Examples include short-term collaboration on projects or long-term investments. Various forms of integration can be distinguished (Figure 50).

The resources which a company invests in entering a strategic alliance depend on its internal reasons for doing so and on its market position (e.g. as market leader). In most cases, more than one other company is involved; this means that there can be a number of different motives, levels of investment

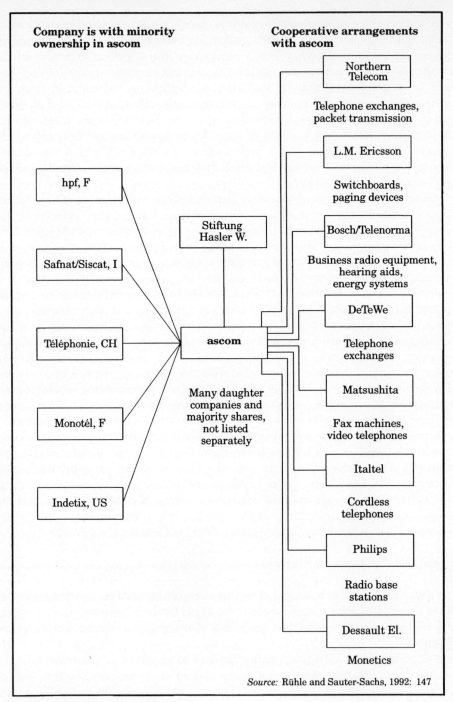

Company is with minority ownership in ascom

Cooperative arrangements with ascom

Northern Telecom

Telephone exchanges, packet transmission

hpf, F

L.M. Ericsson

Switchboards, paging devices

Safnat/Siscat, I

Stiftung Hasler W.

Bosch/Telenorma

Business radio equipment, hearing aids, energy systems

Téléphonie, CH

ascom

DeTeWe

Telephone exchanges

Many daughter companies and majority shares, not listed separately

Matsushita

Monotél, F

Fax machines, video telephones

Italtel

Cordless telephones

Indetix, US

Philips

Radio base stations

Dessault El.

Monetics

Source: Rühle and Sauter-Sachs, 1992: 147

Figure 50 Ascom's strategic alliances.

and (internal) goals, and different measures of success. A strategic alliance is not an end in itself, but rather a means of development, of gaining access to new markets, and of learning and internalizing management processes. The most important feature of a venture of this kind will be not the simple optimization of profit, but learning. A joint venture should not be regarded as an ongoing conflict. It is more like a child growing up. Children need a certain length of time in which to mature and learn to lead their own lives. During this time, there is constant sharing of knowledge between parents and child, and a continuous process of learning.

The use of strategic alliances is a progressive management method which facilitates learning as well as growth. The experience of founding and building up an alliance can increase the capacity for action. Lorange and Roos (1992) consider it a mistake to underestimate the unique knowledge gained through strategic alliances, since it complements general management practices.

Strategic alliances offer unique opportunities for exploiting the advantages of global strategies and international size and scope; at the same time, they can act locally enough to build up acceptance. Ownership and responsibility are shared worldwide. A transnational network of this kind may be *the* organizational form of the future.

In May 1990, Swissair joined Austrian Airlines and SAS to form the European Quality Alliance (EQA). The company joined this alliance because its home market was small and its position in Europe therefore weak. The alliance offered it the advantages of synergy. Now, thanks to shared passenger and freight services, and combined sales points within EQA, customers are offered a better range of services. Construction and business costs were also reduced.

Learning through alliances and learning within alliances both depend on various constellations within the organizational structure. First, there are the exchanges which take place between two or more different companies within the alliance. These companies have different views, so discussions ensue with the aim of developing shared visions. Interests and opinions internal to the companies are revealed. This opens up new directions, which can then be developed. Secondly, different company cultures meet within an alliance, and may clash. The same happens with people who come from different countries and have been shaped by different cultural influences. This leads to discussion of values and norms, and increases the ability to deal with conflict. Conflict is not always beneficial; however, it may drive the learning process by forcing an exchange of ideas.

Clearly, then, alliances are not just a way of achieving success on global markets: they also promote internal learning processes, which increase the company's capacity for action and problem-solving skills.

Case study 17 ───────────────────

Digital Equipment Enterprise

Digital Equipment Enterprise (DEE) was a young company formed in 1991 by the merging of parts of Mannesman-Kienzle, Philips and Digital Equipment Corporation (Figure 51). Digital Equipment Corporation (DEC) is one of the world's leading computer firms. It is an international company which originated in the USA and which specializes in networked computer systems, software and services.

In 1991, DEC made a strategic decision. At that time, the company dominated the market for institutional users and had a strong market presence in that segment. The company decided to focus on a new market segment, the market for small and medium-sized users, although it lacked know-how in that area.

Once the decision was taken, the next question was how? It soon became obvious that the company lacked the internal skills and the flexibility needed to enter that particular market segment, so alternative methods had to be found. Several previous attempts had failed. To avoid making the same mistakes again, the company's senior management decided to buy parts of Philips and Kienzle. These companies already had access to the markets in question, and were currently operating in them, so entry would be much easier. DEC had previously had problems because of lack of flexibility and the

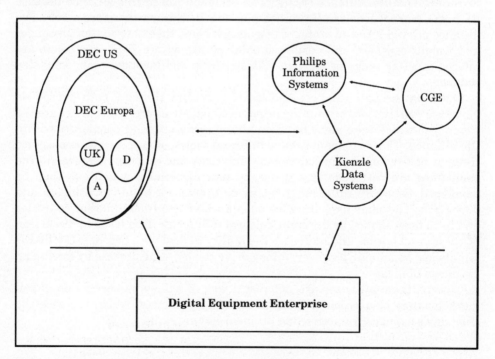

Figure 51 Digital Equipment Enterprise organization.

bureaucratic nature of the company structure. To circumvent these problems, and to avoid high costs, a new organization was founded, called Digital Equipment Enterprise. New management methods and practices were to be applied in this company, in the hope that they would bring the desired success. DEE was an independent and autonomous enterprise which was free to develop in its own way and make its own operational decisions.

As a result of internal restructuring on a global scale, DEE disappeared from most European countries in July 1993. However, DEC had undergone a learning process. What had happened?

During its period of operation, DEE had to perform some new management tasks. It had to harmonize significant aspects of management amongst the companies which had been acquired; this led to an analysis of DEC's management philosophy. *Examination* of the following aspects led to an internal learning process:

- Goals
- Leadership
- Autonomy
- Flexibility
- Redundancy

The *goals* of DEE were not sufficiently clear; this caused the organization to deviate from its purpose. Another factor behind this deviation was the slow rate at which the different company cultures were integrated. This created high potential for conflict supported by a lack of channels of communication.

Levels of *leadership* competence differed amongst individual branches of DEE in different countries. Lack of ability to manage a start-up operation, to deal with conflict and to implement a new company culture hampered the

integration process in some cases.

Although the role of DEE relative to DEC was clear in theory, the degree of actual *autonomy* was uncertain. This led to various delimitation difficulties and conflicts between DEE and DEC. DEE, the younger and smaller organization, was treated like a child and was constantly obliged to make a fuss in order to obtain access to information and resources. It became apparent that clearer limits ought to have been set between the two organizations. Conversely, a network should have been established for the purpose of sharing information and exchanging problem-solving skills; this would have allowed the companies to take advantage of the potential synergy in the system.

Because of its lack of *flexibility* and its complex decision-making process, DEC was unable to react promptly to DEE's requests. One consequence of this was that DEE had to build up large stocks to meet its own customers' orders on time.

Within a year, DEE had succeeded in building up certain management principles and practices which enabled it to integrate the acquired companies. This was DEE's own achievement: DEC offered almost no help during this period, and resource networks were virtually non-existent. There were constant difficulties over the dividing line between DEC and DEE; this led some members of the organization to question why two firms were being developed rather than one. The question of *redundancy* was finally settled by reintegrating DEE into DEC. The following points arise from the evaluation talks.

DEE: lessons learned
If an organization has clear goals, then it is in a better position to meet its

objectives and to avoid misunderstandings, conflicts and difficulties in making decisions. If the theory of action coincides with the theory in use, there is an atmosphere of trust. This enables members of the organization to get on with their jobs without having to struggle with unclear pronouncements and conflicting relationships.

In new companies, different cultures have to be integrated and the proper level of autonomy established. Start-up difficulties call for leadership of a different kind from that needed in companies which are already up and running, and where there are no problems about delimitation or culture. New companies need the kind of management skills which have to take this into account. Selection criteria for management should therefore be re-examined.

The levels of autonomy and control should be made clear from the beginning. Doing so will avoid disastrous escalation of 'border disputes' over customers between the new company and the parent company. Clear definition of the degree of autonomy is essential for successful operation: lack of clarity means that conflicts are 'programmed in' from the outset. The need for a network of resources and problem-solving skills was identified as a critical factor.

Decision-making processes and mechanisms for resolving conflicts must be discussed, and adapted if necessary. The settlement of conflicts between organizations should give rise to attitudes of acceptance and flexibility towards different internal management principles.

The transfer of knowledge throughout the whole organization is an important factor in successful learning. A knowledge network can serve as a basis for successful management of future acquisitions and sharing of problem-solving strategies. By reflecting on the process of managing DEE, DEC was able to learn from its experience. Lessons learned helped to initiate the third level of learning — process learning, or learning to learn.

10

Learning by developing
a culture

1 The cultural context

Culture is a system of knowledge and insights which serve as a basis for interpreting experiences and generating actions (Klimecki and Probst, 1990). Culture is an 'implicit phenomenon', and is expressed in shared values, norms and attitudes. Management activity cannot be considered independently of culture because it is culture which sets the pattern of meanings within which actions are taken, evaluated and explained. Internal and external interactions give rise to a frame of reference which members of the organization use when making interpretations. This frame of reference is frequently shared, and provides a way of categorizing the actions and perceptions of the organization. However, culture is not only the framework of the whole system but also the product of the system as a whole.

Learning may be seen as the preparation of a new cultural framework. Learning implies both a need to change frames of reference and to allow a diversity of values and norms to emerge. The development of culture is therefore a fertile ground for organizational learning. From this point of view, it is the procedural aspect of culture development which is important. This is an aspect which is not often emphasized. Shaping culture so as to promote organizational learning can be seen in terms of cultivating processes and transmitting meaning.

We regard the development of culture as the preparation of material and symbolic contexts for making interpretations. Such contexts may include forms of language, ceremonies, communication processes, and the development of

Development of vision and mission statements	Who: Managers (elite) and groups Aim: Analysis of values, norms and goals
Communication fora	Who: Individuals and groups Aim: Analysis of values and norms
Image analyses	Who: Members of the organization Aim: Analysis of values and norms

Figure 52 Culture development as a learning process.

vision and mission statements and leadership principles. We now use examples to illustrate the cultural context for learning processes. The development of vision and mission statements, the analysis of a company image and the processes of communication are all aids to the development of a culture conducive to learning (Figure 52).

2 Development of vision and mission statements

A company's vision and mission statement contains a clear listing and definition of its permanent values and aims as an institution. It serves as a framework for behaviour and for the way that people see themselves (Probst, 1993). However, it is not just the content of the vision and mission statement which is of interest, it is the process of its development which leads to learning. The vision and mission statement, and the way in which it is introduced and applied within the company, help to determine the company culture. It is particularly important that many of the members of the company participate to formulate the content. This can only happen as a result of group processes in which members of the organization develop a shared vision. This determines how the vision is interpreted, what opportunities and risks it implies, and what limits it sets. Its main task is to convey meaning.

The development of the vision and mission statement thus helps to give an identity to the system, to create meaning, and to mould or influence the culture of the organization. This happens as a result of group processes in which members work together to construct a collective view of the reality of their everyday life. The outcome is a meaningful context in which all the actions of the system can be set. It is the basis of the feelings of identity and the 'we-feeling' of the people in the organization; these are probably the main reasons for having a company culture. Culture conveys meaning, sets the framework for action and serves as a normative grid for orientation purposes.

We may now ask how the development of a vision and mission statement can serve organizational learning. Internal and external interactions trigger a process of reflection, during which the network of values, norms, beliefs and normative attitudes is analyzed. This can lead to existing goals being changed or adapted. The development of a vision and mission statement is thus a potential instrument changing frames of reference, and it can at the same time be the basis of a shared culture.

The extent to which the principles contained in the vision and mission statement can actually be applied in the everyday life of a company depends largely on the extent to which the formulations are accepted. If the members of the organization can identify with the content of the statement at the development stage, it is very likely that it will form a cultural framework within which organizational learning takes place.

Example: Vision and mission statements

Vision and mission statements consist of basic orientations and long-term aims and guidelines. They usually state the company's intentions and values in respect of business achievement, social dimensions and leadership. As an example, we look at the vision statement of Ciba-Geigy in the early 1990s.

VISION STATEMENT OF CIBA-GEIGY

Our Vision

By striking a balance between our economic, social and environmental responsibilities, we want to ensure the prosperity of our enterprise beyond the year 2000.

1. *Responsibility for long-term economic success*
We aim to generate appropriate financial results through sustainable growth and constant renewal of a balanced business structure, so that we justify the confidence of all those who rely on our company — stockholders, employees, business partners and the public.

We will not put our long-term future in danger by taking short-term profits.

2. *Social responsibility*
Ciba-Geigy is open and trustworthy towards society. Through our business activities we wish to make a worthwhile contribution to the solution of global issues and to the progress of mankind.

We recognize our responsibility when turning new discoveries in science and technology into commercial reality; we carefully evaluate benefits and risks in all our activities, processes and products.

3. *Responsibility for the environment*
Respect for the environment must be part of everything we do. We design products and processes to fulfil their purpose safely and with as little environmental impact as possible. We use natural resources and energy in the best possible way and reduce waste in all forms.

It is our duty to dispose safely of all unavoidable waste using state-of-the-art technology.

Leadership

Living up to our three equal-ranking reponsibilities requires enlightened and determined leadership.

Our leaders set examples. They must have vision, courage, human concern, and a sense of reality.

We believe in Directed Autonomy — giving direction to our employees while allowing them the authority and the flexibility they need to accomplish their tasks.

We encourage and reward an entrepreneurial, risk-taking behaviour in our employees.

Customer orientation The customer is the focus of everything we do	We provide value to our customers by combining products, information and services that allow them to improve their performance. We strive to make Ciba-Geigy their business partner of choice.
Innovation The creative spirit of our employees is vital to our business	We are open to change, and we constantly look for opportunities to innovate. We allow room for expression and failures. Innovative behaviour in all fields is recognized and rewarded.
Quality We are committed to quality	Quality to us means that we continually meet mutually agreed requirements within the company, between Ciba-Geigy employees, as well as in all our dealings with business partners and society in general.
Organization We organize for responsiveness and flexibility	Our organization is based on largely autonomous Business Units with an integral and worldwide responsibility for their particular mission. The Executive Committee and Business Units' headquarters provide strategic management while responsibility and authority for operational activities are decentralized. Group Companies provide an optimal framework and guidance for local operations.
Market leadership We reach for sustainable competitive advantage	Based on our scientific, technical and marketing competence, we strive to be among the leaders in all the markets we choose to become involved in.
Sustainable growth We develop a competitive edge through qualitative growth	We look for long-term sustainable growth, i.e. profitable expansion of our business with products and services that exhibit superior benefit/risk ratios and bring about reduced resource consumption as well as reduced waste per unit.
Integrity Trust, fairness and honesty	are the basics for our relationship with stakeholders and we respect acknowledged ethical standards. We provide current, continuous and honest information and engage in an open dialogue with the public.

| **People relationships**
People build the company's success | We encourage people to grow — professionally and personally — to their highest level, regardless of sex, colour, nationality or religious beliefs. Through recognition in decision-making, we build a sense of purpose in our people so that they are prepared to give their best. |
| **Product benefits**
Our products must contribute to the satisfaction of real needs | Our products and services add value in agriculture, health care and a wide variety of industries, and they improve the quality of life of individuals. |

In 1996, Ciba-Geigy merged with Sandoz. The two firms have adopted the new name Novartis. By developing a new vision and mission statement, a learning process bridging existing cultural differences (Ciba-Geigy: participative, long-term orientation *vs* Sandoz: hierarchical, short-term orientation) might be initiated within Novartis.

Case study 18

Swisscontrol

In a project carried out by Swisscontrol, the development of a vision and mission statement was used as a way of finding an identity and creating guidelines for renewed thinking and action of the company (Probst, 1989). Swisscontrol was one of three new companies formed on 1 January 1988 from Radio Switzerland Ltd. Swisscontrol — or Swiss Flight Safety Ltd — is responsible for the safe and economic execution of civil aviation in Swiss airspace and from the following airports: Zürich Kloten, Geneva Cointrin, Bern Belp and Lugano. In 1980, the air traffic controllers dealt with about 1.2 million flights a year in controlled airspace; during daily peak hours, there can be up to 1,300 flights. In 1988, Swisscontrol had 1,800 employees.

In 1988, Swisscontrol was labouring under considerable pressure. The reasons for this were internal structural changes, together with external flight safety problems arising from the increased volume of air traffic. Productivity, quality, safety and economy were all of vital importance. To enable the organization to deal satisfactorily with all these issues, its orientation and its boundaries needed clear definition.

The process of developing a vision and mission statement was intended to bring values into the open and to help formulate guidelines for the future. If a company is to have a direction, it needs a common framework which is kept under constant review. If people are to make sense of events, concentrate their efforts, and decide and act meaningfully within a collective system, they need a vision. It must be a vision which employees can share and understand. Activities are channelled and developed by reference to the company guidelines or goals. The first step in developing a vision and mission statement is to find a meaning in the tasks which have to be performed and in the connected responsibilities.

How can a vision and mission statement be developed to suit a whole company? To ensure a common framework, as many employees as possible ought to take part in the development process. The vision and mission statement is not just a matter for senior management; it should determine the orientation of all members of the organization. The vision must be part of people's lives, and must be seen to affect everyone directly. The process of developing the vision and mission statement ought to be accompanied by the planning of a set of practical measures, so that the direct effect of the vision becomes clear (Figure 53).

The first item in the vision and mission statement should be a statement of company goals. This should include general aims and the company's *raison d'être*. The values of the company are then stated; however, the main emphasis here is not on the values themselves, but on the ways in which they are expressed, the opportunities for putting them into practice, and the intended courses of action. The aim is to describe the general policy aims of the company with regard to finance, productivity, social matters and management. It is important to plan measures at this stage for putting shared values into effect.

An important feature of the development process is that participants should reach agreement on suggested values. Reaching an agreement presupposes questioning and critical analysis, which are important learning activities as they provide an opportunity to examine existing behaviour patterns

and to set changes in motion if necessary. Even when the vision and mission statement has been completed, it should be kept under continuous review and adapted as appropriate. Analysis and continuous monitoring are essential if higher-level learning is to take place.

The following aspects of the process of developing a vision and mission statement can contribute to organizational learning.

1. Uniqueness of vision and mission statement

Completed vision and mission statements may look similar, but they differ in the ways in which they are developed, perceived and interpreted in each company.

2. Participation

Top management must be involved because of the strategic nature of the vision and mission statement. However, this does not mean that all other employees are to be excluded. On the contrary, they must be kept in touch with the vision and mission statement and its development, and they should form project groups to interpret its implications for their own activities. Without this kind of participation, the vision and mission statement is usually just a document, and its contents are rarely implemented. It is important, therefore, that people should be able to identify with the vision and mission statement.

3. Forward-looking nature

Another important aspect of the vision and mission statement is what it says about the future. Although no-one can decide where the company is heading until the current business environment has been analyzed, future opportunities

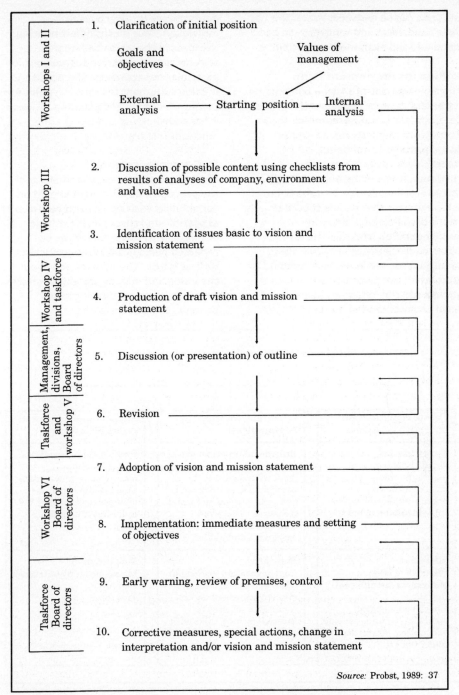

Source: Probst, 1989: 37

Figure 53 Development process of a vision and mission statement.

and risks can be deduced. When this has been done, ideas and solutions can be combined and examined for feasibility.

4. Plan for implementation

The development of a vision and mission statement must be accompanied by the development of measures which show its practical implications, and make participants feel confident that something is really happening. However, it should be borne in mind that everything cannot be done at once. It is important that people should be aware of the possible delay in implementation, and that this is reflected in their expectations. Basic conditions for implementation should be established and priorities set. Implementation proceeds by means of small projects carried out in departments or by groups or individuals. This means differentiating the ideas in the vision and mission statement into concrete suggestions for particular departments. The vision and mission statement is a starting-point for setting objectives and planning actions; it has coordinating and integrating functions (Figure 54).

5. Communication

The vision and mission statement and the process of developing it should be communicated as openly and realistically as possible and through all available channels. This procedure must be repeated periodically. It is a critical success factor. The information about the vision and mission statement should cover background, development, content, consequences and

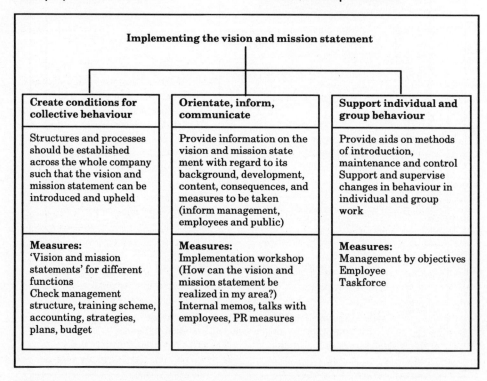

Figure 54 Implementing the vision and mission statement

implementation procedures (e.g. workshops in individual departments). The development and implementation processes must be accompanied by a suitable and honest information policy. Top management has the important task of living the content of the vision and mission statement from the beginning, and thus communicating it by example.

6. Innovation
The vision and mission statement must contain an innovative element. Its development must be seen as a change in the frame of reference. The majority of participants in the development process must recognize some change in the general orientation. In other words, the development of the vision and mission statement must be a real stimulus for change.

7. Monitoring
Early warning systems and the process of monitoring implementation provide a check on the initial premises. The company needs to know whether the basic assumptions are still valid or whether they have already changed. Decisions were based on certain descriptions of situations: are these descriptions still accurate? Are the constructed scenarios still meaningful? Present activities need to be checked to see whether they accord with the vision and mission statement. The aim is to achieve effective and efficient implementation of the vision and mission statement (Probst, 1989).

Case study 19

Gore & Associates Inc.

Gore & Associates was founded in 1958 by William Gore for the purpose of marketing PTFE (polytetrafluoroethylene). Gore had previously worked for Du Pont de Nemours. During his time there, he had been employed in research and development, and had come up with a new product: ribbon cable coated with PTFE. Gore discussed the product with Du Pont, but the company was not interested in marketing it. He therefore founded his own company to manufacture PFTE-related products, the best known of which is Gore-tex.

In 1990, Gore & Associates had a turnover of US$660 million. Its success is due primarily to the chemical composition of PTFE; however, it may also be partly attributable to the fact that the company shows a number of features of a learning organization.

Gore & Associates functions without titles, hierarchies or any of the structures normally found in companies of comparable size. Its management style has often been described as 'unmanagement'. Gore believes that formal management techniques put a brake on individual creativity. He has said that the goal of the company is 'to make money and have fun', and to do so by 'being able to do what you want to do rather than do what somebody else tells you to do'.

Viewed as a learning organization, there are four features of Gore's company which are of special significance:

- The size of the production sites
- The fact that the company works with associates
- The lattice style of the organization

■ The four principles upon which the Gore philosophy is based.

Together these features have led to a company culture which can be described as a learning organization.

The production sites were to be small: the number of employees working at each site was not to exceed 400. The policy of working with associates is an integral part of the company's philosophy, as can be seen from its name. However, it is the third feature, i.e. the lattice organization, which is essential from the point of view of organizational learning.

Gore & Associates has been described not only as 'unmanaged', but also as unstructured. It has also been described as having a lattice structure, i.e. a structure with the following characteristics:

■ Direct lines of communication, person-to-person
■ No fixed allocation of responsibility
■ Use of sponsors
■ Use of natural leadership
■ Setting of objectives by the people who have to 'make them happen'
■ Organization of tasks and functions by means of commitments.

Bill Gore said: 'Every successful organization has an underground lattice. It's where the news spreads like lightning, where people can go around the organization to get things done.'

This kind of structure can only exist where the number of employees working together is quite small. The size of the site has therefore been an important factor in Gore's style of management. The organizational structure has been likened to an amoeba because its shape constantly changes. The shape does not matter, so long as the objectives are met.

The four principles underlying the Gore philosophy form the culture which holds the company together as a learning organization. Starting from his basic philosophy, 'to make money and have fun', Gore derived four principles: freedom, commitment, fairness and discretion. The last of these has also been called the 'water-line principle', by analogy with a ship: the vessel is in much greater danger from a hole below the water-line than from one above it. In practice, discretion meant that the company had no travel policy or expenses reports: individuals are expected to act in a cost-conscious manner.

The four aspects of the company which we have described in this section are the qualities which make Gore & Associates into a learning organization. It is the combination of these four that created the culture of learning. Developing this culture was crucial if Gore was to become a learning organization.

3 Communication fora

Communication is the transfer of information between individuals, groups or systems which use it in the further development of their codes (Lutz, 1991). This means that people in organizations use communication to develop cultural norms and values and to perceive changes. We may ask what is meant by the word 'code' in this context. According to Lutz (1991: 104), it is the 'set of items of information which decides which part of its environment an organism perceives, and how (perceptual filter) the information, once selected, is weighed and evaluated; how far the organism uses the information in its further development (e.g. to extend its mental model of reality); and what outward actions (signals, physical acts) the organism performs as a result of it (the code determines the available patterns of action and expression)'. The code is described in terms such as genetic code, personality and culture, which are taken from biology, psychology and sociology. The code provides information on the nature of the environment, about itself and about behaviours which are successful in the environment.

Communication fora facilitate organizational learning because their function is to develop such codes, and this involves questioning existing norms and values. The codes of individual participants are enriched and changed during the communication process. This gives rise to new frames of reference, which are a collective view jointly developed by people within a social system.

It is important to realize that it is only through *communication* within and between individuals that each can identify with their job and with the company. Communication also enables people to develop a collective view of reality. High-quality internal communication brings transparency into company life and helps to integrate complex relationships so that people gain a wider view of the whole system. Learning is aided by communication by permitting the identification of principles and values and increasing the sharing of information.

Example: Analysis of assumptions

All decisions and actions are based on assumptions. People often act based on the assumption that things will be the same in the future as they were in the past, that people are all alike, that everybody thinks the same and wants the same, that people make rational decisions, that organizations are structured to be effective, that it is easy for customers to tell whether a product is useful to them, and so on. In other words, people make basic assumptions almost without question. It is difficult to see why, because the opposites of all the assumptions listed might just as easily be true.

Communications fora are a good way of establishing a common basis for challenging assumptions and making decisions. They give participants a chance to test their existing assumptions; to work together to redevelop assumptions, norms and values, and thus to lay a foundation for working together in the future (Kilmann, 1984: 139 ff).

Analyzing assumptions is a way of questioning organizational norms and values which facilitates organizational learning. In the course of discussions in and between groups, alternative explanations and different views emerge, and these can then be examined and tested for validity. This activity triggers a learning process. Analysis of assumptions is often an established feature of strategic controlling which leads to learning (Probst and Gomez, 1991).

Analysis of assumptions usually involves six steps:

- Developing strategic alternatives and their implications
- Assignment of groups to the different alternatives
- Analysis of assumptions within groups
- Analysis of assumptions amongst groups
- Dissolving and resynthesizing assumptions
- Establishing a joint conclusion (Kilmann, 1984: 144)

Following these steps ought to reveal basic assumptions and point the way towards learning how to change.

Case study 20

Volkswagen Ltd

As an example, we look at how Volkswagen carries out an analysis of assumptions in order to develop a strategic plan for the twenty-first century.

Step 1
The company must choose among the following options:

- Concentrate on the production of 'economical' cars, and stay in competition with foreign producers
- Specialize in the original idea of 'a small car for all people'
- Diversify into other kinds of vehicle, e.g. lorries, electric cars
- Diversify into other markets to compensate for the fluctuating cycles in the car industry

These extreme positions emphasize the differences between the alternatives and form the basis for the analysis of assumptions described below.

Step 2
Volkswagen chooses about fifty employees from different functions, e.g.

marketing, production, research and development, and some people outside the company. Each person is assigned to the strategic alternative of his or her own choice. This provides the basis for the analysis.

Step 3
Lists are made of all the internal and external factors which affect the different strategies. A list is then made of 5–10 assumptions which support the conclusion (e.g. there will be no revival in the car industry in the near future; foreign competition is increasing). The following questions are then put to the group: Are the assumptions balanced? Are the assumptions realistic? The safe assumptions can be distinguished from the unsafe ones, and the important from the less important. The results can be entered in a matrix (Figure 55).

Step 4
After each group has discussed its own assumptions, the groups share their findings. Each group must present its assumptions for questioning; this leads to an open discussion. As a result of this

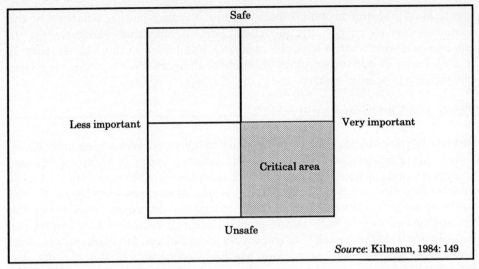

Source: Kilmann, 1984: 149

Figure 55 Matrix for positioning assumptions.

discussion, the groups may make changes to the assumptions on which they are working.

In the case of Volkswagen, it is difficult to say which of the alternatives offers the best chance of success. It is nevertheless important that the assumptions are examined, to initiate the learning process.

Step 5
After each group has had a chance to change its assumptions and present them again, a new 'synthesizing' group is formed. The purpose of this group is to analyze and interpret the current assumptions in the course of a dialogue.

Step 6
This dialogue leads to a final decision on the assumptions. The results are given in the form of an assumptions matrix, prepared by all the groups.

The process of analyzing assumptions gives the participants an opportunity to reveal and share information. It is therefore part of an organizational learning process. Individual perceptions of reality are made accessible to all and are examined. The sharing of information is a chance to arrive at a collective view. This makes it easier to identify the underlying norms and values.

4 Company climate

The company climate has been recognized as an important factor affecting work. One reason for this is that as structures collapse, the working climate is important as a source of identity. Companies often behave as systems which create stability, and in which working and learning merge. Analysis of the company climate plays an important part in locating shortcomings in employees' identification with the company, and hence in their motivation. It is also a way of making employees aware of their own perceptions, and thus triggering a process of reflection.

Example: The image analysis

Studies of company image can be of great value as early warning indicators. Two kinds of image are often studied: the external image (held by society and customers) and the internal image (how the employees see the company?). Image profiles help the company not only to ascertain its position but also to analyze itself or to make timely changes and introduce corrective measures. The perceptions of people both inside and outside the company affect customer satisfaction, sales, the quality of employees potential and job applicants. It does not matter whether the perceptions are justified or not. In this context, the truth is whatever people believe. When measuring customer satisfaction, therefore, it is important to reach agreement on the meaning of the results and not to react to disappointment with mere excuses. It is vital to analyze and

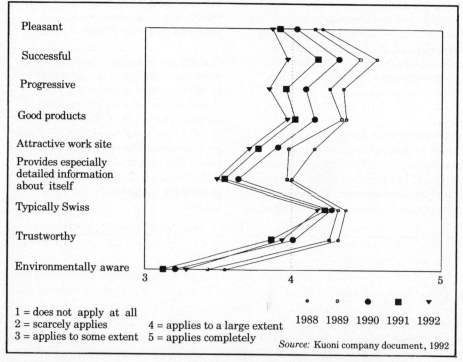

Figure 56 Example of an image barometer in Kuoni: average profiles 1988–92

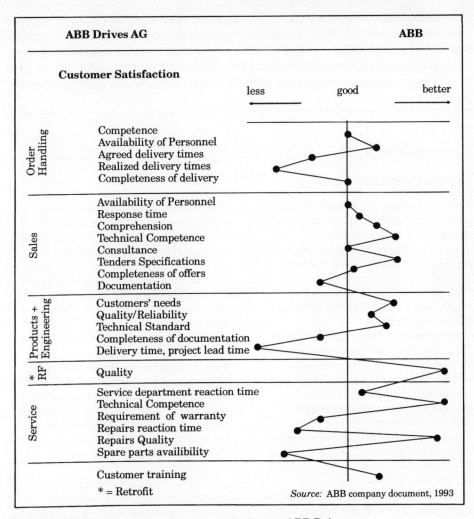

Figure 57 Measurement of customer satisfaction at ABB Drives.

discuss the results, and to highlight the major features which are revealed. People must be made aware of these features so that knowledge can be increased and action triggered.

In Kuoni, Hewlett-Packard and ABB, image radar systems are assessment tools used to initiate learning processes. Whenever strategic development is being planned, Kuoni analyzes the results of image studies, uses them as the basis for benchmarking and adopts appropriate measures (Figure 56). In ABB, the Customer Focus programme has given special importance to image measurement. The measurement of customer satisfaction has a vital radar function. ABB Drives uses the data listed in Figure 57 to measure customer satisfaction.

Within ABB, it was found that it is easier and cheaper to maintain or improve customer satisfaction than to attract new customers or win back old ones. Again, the investigations are organized into a whole programme of recording, evaluation, analysis, and determination of priorities and plans for action. It is the entire programme rather than the individual stages which prompts learning processes.

Case study 21

Hewlett-Packard Ltd

Hewlett-Packard (Germany) Ltd is an information technology company which specializes in the production of equipment for measurement and data processing. It is the largest overseas branch of the American concern. In 1985, Hewlett-Packard (Germany) carried out an analysis of its external and internal images.

The Hewlett-Packard philosophy is that a company can only be successful if all its employees work together to achieve the company goals. These goals, which ought to be shared by all members of the company, must be realistic; they must be understood by every employee; and they must reflect the essential character of the company. The basic policies are to employ able and creative people, to stimulate enthusiasm and motivation amongst the employees, and to facilitate integration and cooperation.

Hewlett-Packard believes that satisfied and motivated employees are the most effective and productive, and that it is therefore in the best interest of the company to have a good internal image. A regular internal survey was therefore initiated in 1985. The slogan 'Employees speak out' was adopted, and employees were asked to give honest answers to a variety of questions. The results of the survey occupy an important place in the company culture.

They are regarded as a source of information on the internal state of Hewlett-Packard and, most importantly, as an aid to comparing actual and projected fulfilment of company goals. Employees are deliberately involved in the process of learning about changes in the image, and about the problems which are revealed.

The internal image barometer shows what the company climate is like and how it might be improved (Figure 58). The results are communicated to the employees in special reports, with comments by the managing director and personnel manager (*OpenLine*, an in-house magazine of HP). This is an important aspect of using image barometers.

Within the image measurement process, the amount of learning is limited. Significant learning processes begin at the stage where feedback groups analyze the results, examine problem areas and make plans. Groups are established in different areas of the company to evaluate the problems in detail and to suggest feasible solutions. Some employees receive special training in analysis and interpretation and are then integrated into the groups. The solutions produced by the groups are to lead to changes. They are asked to produce answers to the following questions:

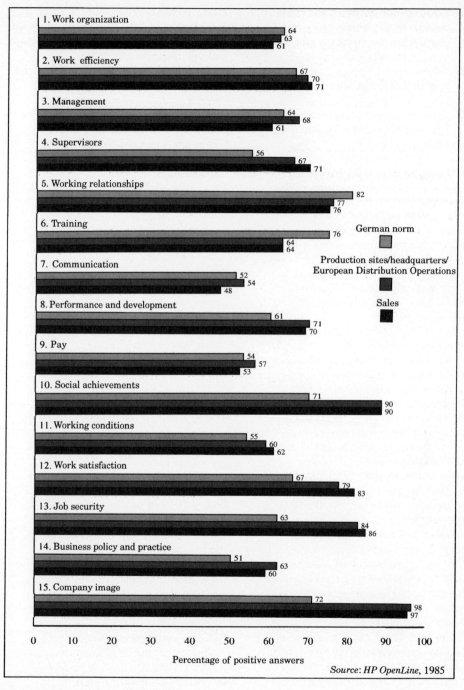

Figure 58 Extract from HP survey.

- Which of our decisions and goals need to be explained, and which concepts in our company culture need to be clarified?
- Where would we like to make an improvement but are unable to do so?
- Where do we want to make changes? How and why would we do it?

Learning processes are set in motion by the repeated examination of the internal image, the feedback given to employees and the teamwork involved in finding possible solutions. The image survey is simply a source of information. It is the feedback and the group analysis of norms and values which prompt reflection on the company goals. These activities serve to build up a collective view of reality. They are also a deliberate way of initiating and supporting learning processes.

11

Learning by developing human resources

1 The human resource context

Human interactions form the basis of organizational activity and set the framework for organizational learning. We shall therefore look at human resource management as a vital element in the learning process. Our discussion will focus not on the training of individuals in the traditional sense, but on interactive processes. The communication skills of individuals and their desire for self-development are merely media of organizational learning. It is only when personal values, interests and demands are connected that organizational learning can occur. One of the main tasks of human resource managers is to nurture employees' interactive skills so as to promote organizational learning. The emphasis is on participative, group-oriented learning. The group, which is a unit consisting of two or more persons, functions as a catalyst between the individual and the organization: the knowledge of the individual can be transmitted through various groups (autonomous groups, learning partnerships, etc.).

It is important from the point of view of organizational learning that employees are helped to increase their intercultural, communication and participation skills. We now consider some forms of interaction which facilitate organizational learning. We concentrate on learning partnerships, on-the-job interventions, and mapping.

2 Learning partnerships

Learning processes within organizations usually involve interaction between individuals. It is important, therefore, to consider members of the organization and their relationships, and to analyze the contribution which these relationships make to organizational learning (Figure 59).

Given the increasing complexity and the dynamic nature of the environment, learning cannot be simply a matter of internal training programmes. The problems of transfer of learning and provision of training by outside agencies need to be handled differently. How can the education and training department teach employees to turn concepts into action? There is a growing demand for human resource development and organizational development to be combined in one integrated process, so that learning becomes part of working. The distinction between teaching and learning ought to disappear in favour of 'making learning natural' (Sattelberger, 1991b). Similarly, the classical distinction between individual development and organizational development will also have to disappear, so that the two can be integrated.

New ways of learning will be needed if individual learning and organizational learning are to be combined in the work setting. Learning partnerships need to be part of the everyday life of the company. They can override the traditional system of work division and enable collective learning to take place.

Learning partnerships take different forms, notably coaching, mentoring and development alliances. The key features of all these forms of partnership are that they are interpersonal relationships within organizations and that they are based on exchange. The processes which take place within the relationship include a broadening of perceptions and awareness, assimilation of new information, and the development of new personal frames of references.

Figure 60 shows the forms of partnership described by Sattelberger (1991a), based on Megginson (1988). They differ in focus, duration, method and outcomes. They are all examples of interpersonal relationships which can lead to a change in behaviour as a result of identifying and analyzing values and norms.

Learning partnerships	Who: Individuals and groups Aim: Interchange and analysis of values and norms
On-the-job interventions	Who: All members of the organization Aim: Intergration of work and learning
Cognitive mapping	Who: Individuals and groups Aim: Analysis of values and norms

Figure 59 Human resource development as a learning process.

Comparison of instruction, coaching and mentoring			
Action by supervisor / Dimension	Instruction	Coaching	Mentoring
Focus	Specific task	Longer-term work outcome	Development of individual
Duration	One or two days	From one month to one year	Whole career or lifetime
Type of assistance	Explaining, showing, instructing, checking, giving feedback	Working together through problems or situations with the aim of acquiring or trying out new skills	Being a friend and partner: listening, asking questions and defending different positions so as to increase the range of awareness of the other person
Intended benefits to the learner	Predictable and standardizable performance on a given task at a given time	Increased ability to work independently and to find creative solutions to new problems	Analysis of previous assumptions about roles at work and in life, and clarification of future directions
Possible outcomes for the helper	Satisfaction and control of standards	Satisfaction because learner shows motivation and initiative in his/her development	Questions for the mentor himself/ herself; fulfilment

Source: Sattelberger, 1991a: 210

Figure 60 Examples of learning partnerships.

Example: Human resource development alliances

A human resource development alliance is an alliance between members of a company, regardless of their position, each of whom has an interest in his or her own development and in the development of the organization. An alliance is created when expectations are agreed and put into (written) contracts. With regard to content, the alliance can cover all kinds of themes, from work-specific problems through tasks within the organization to personal problems.

Human resource development alliances may take the form of coaching or of mentoring. Coaching deals mainly with particular aspects of work, whereas mentoring is concerned with an individual's whole career. Coaching is appropriate in the following situations:

- Preparation for first or new leadership position
- Working abroad
- Working on challenging and innovative projects
- Assessment procedures

Mentoring is appropriate for:

- Surviving a culture shock
- Establishing a balance between work and private life
- Preparation for retirement

Once the content of the relationship has been decided, agreement is reached on the aims and duration of the relationship, and on expectations, ways of meeting objectives, exchange of information and expected benefits. An alliance should normally last until each of the partners can see a personal gain. An alliance can be set up between any two people regardless of position, age, sex, cultural differences and functional area. The important point is the mutual exchange of information, leading to an analysis of norms and values, and thus stimulating higher-level organizational learning.

Case study 22

Digital Equipment Corporation

Core groups are a form of human resource development alliance which is used in Digital Equipment Corporation (DEC). These groups provide a setting in which values can be analyzed and theories in use can be directly compared with official theories of action. Core groups depend on the voluntary participation of members of the organization who differ with respect to culture, sex, position in the hierarchy or other variables. The voluntary nature of participation enables members to recognize their own limits and those of the organization, and to see ways of overcoming them.

In DEC, a core group usually consists of no more than sixteen people. It is composed of pairs of people who share a common attribute (e.g. two French people, two women, two homosexuals, etc.). The group meets with a neutral person within the organization for a whole day every month to talk about problems which people experience in working with others. The aim of the programme is to break down value-judgements about particular groups of people so as to create a prejudice-free atmosphere in which people can work together. The core groups compel groups of people within the organization to examine their own values and to create a new basis for future work.

3 On-the-job interventions

Organizational learning may be stimulated by increasing employees' active involvement in their work. For Argyris (1990), the most important factor is the breaking down of organizational defensive routines. The idea behind this approach is to use the skills and abilities of individuals in such a way that they can work effectively without the authority of a superior. Since people have a learning potential which is hardly ever fully exploited, it seems probable that active, on-the-job learning programmes could teach employees to think in different ways. Organizational defensive patterns can be broken down if work and learning are integrated in participative, on-the-job activities. This is an important method of breaking down obsolete behaviours.

Organizational learning does mean, however, learning by the whole organization; it cannot be equated with learning by isolated individuals. Organizations have rules, institutions, routines, roles and schemata which dictate 'correct' ways of acting. One of the aims of organizational learning is to change these formal aspects. Where large numbers of people have to relate to each other and coordinate their activities, rules are needed to make actions follow a certain pattern of expectations. The members of the organization use this pattern as a means of orientation. According to Neuberger (1991), these expectations must be formalized (in standardized and written form); generalized in terms of time, social aspects and content; and they should be binding. This will lead to people behaving in predictable ways in the future, and it will help new personnel to know what is expected. All measures for human resource development which provide a framework are welcomed. It is not enough that individuals are prepared to revise particular behaviour patterns; conditions must be created which will permit continuous learning.

The following human resource measures are examples of work-based structures which provide a *framework for learning*:

- The *rotation principle*, which combats narrow networks, possessive thinking, departmental blindness, 'group-think', etc., thus opening the way for new insights.
- *Project work*, carried out by groups which are constantly reconstituted so that different norms, values, opinions, views and suggestions will be brought together. Projects break through hierarchies and departmental barriers, and permit open exchange of different points of view.
- A *forum for suggestions and innovations*, in addition to the formal procedures. This provides a channel for suggestions for change, thus encouraging creative ideas.
- Changes in the *payments and incentive systems* (pay, promotion, working conditions, status symbols) to reward innovative solutions to problems and creative suggestions for the future. (Neuberger, 1991.)

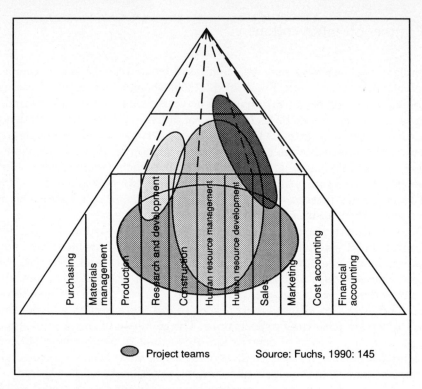

Figure 61 Project teams as a medium for learning.

Example: Learning-oriented project work

Projects are tasks which occupy a limited period of time and which are generally carried out in addition to routine tasks. They involve specialists from different functional areas. Just as the company needs an internal order to be able to function, organizational learning needs a framework in which it can be brought to fruition. Projects are frameworks within which people can work together to solve problems confronting the organization.

There are situations in which the optimal decision is unlikely to be made because all the information has not been considered. In these situations, it is important to establish the best possible framework for learning, taking into account the objectives and the abilities of the people involved. Since the members of the project team come from different functional areas, they bring with them a variety of viewpoints, opinions and suggestions. This reduces the likelihood of information being omitted (Figure 61).

It is not surprising that the differences in viewpoint amongst the members of an interdisciplinary team lead to the questioning of objectives, which may then

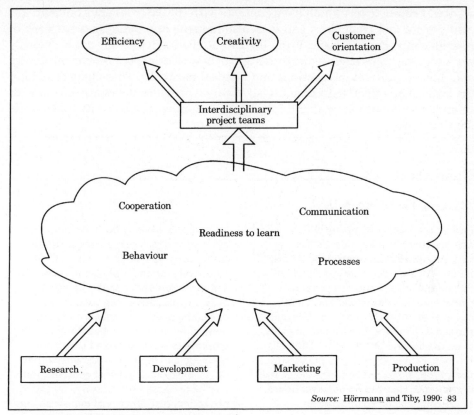

Figure 62 Multidisciplinary project teams.

be redefined. In group projects, existing patterns of behaviour are confronted and analyzed, and attempts are made to find the best solution. This is a particularly important feature, since it increases the problem-solving potential.

In order for projects to be effective, the work process needs to be reflected and agreed upon (see Probst, 1989, and page 109 ff of this book). Figure 62 shows the methodological support of project work which can create suitable conditions for learning. Subsequent steps are concerned with the actual process of solving the problems. This process too should be organized in such a way that learning is initiated and supported. Suitable procedures include networks for thinking and analyzing, playing with models and scenarios, analyzing the rules of the system and establishing early warning systems (Probst, 1993). These procedures lead to analysis of existing rules and norms and to the creation of interactions which prepare the way for higher-level learning.

Project groups can also provide the organization with feedback. The project team is a fresh combination of people who, as a group, can judge the internal and external functioning of the organization from a previously unconsidered point of view. Project teams which have contacts with the external environment, e.g. conferences and trade fairs can increase dialogue and build up a network of relationships. Project teams bring people into contact who did not previously work together; this leads to the formation of new relationships of various kinds, and thus to informal interactions and internal networks. These networks form the basis of an effective feedback system which provides the organization with information about external and internal functioning, and so contributes to its development.

Case study 23

Oticon Holding A/S

Oticon is a Danish company which manufactures hearing aids. Its net turnover in 1994 amounted to DK 750 million; this yielded a net profit of DK 88 million. In 1994 the company had thirteen main sales offices and 1,192 employees. It was founded in 1904, and started to produce its own hearing aids after the Second World War. The business remained in family ownership until 1956. It was not until the latter half of the 1980s that the Foundation Board of Oticon decided to update the company and to appoint new management. In 1986, the new CEO decided to make Oticon into a learning organization.

The new CEO developed a vision aimed at the creation of a company 'where the biggest part of what we are doing is something we are good at and like', 'organized in such a way that all employees working there understand what they are doing', 'where there are as few limits as possible to stop people from doing a good and effective job' and 'where each one of us has many opportunities to develop in the long term, to change working tasks, to try bigger challenges'.

Prompted by growing market pressures and high operating costs, the CEO asked each employee to examine

his own job, looking both for things he did well and for areas where he felt he could learn new skills. It was no longer acceptable for an employee in research and development to spend 25 per cent or less of his time doing 'real' research, or for the product manager to spend none of his time visiting customers. All employees were expected to analyze their job and identify areas where they might make an additional contribution.

The proposed solution was intended not to increase functional expertise but rather to maximize the contribution made by individuals to the organization as a whole. This meant that when activities in one area were behind schedule, employees from other areas would be available to give extra help. The company redesigned itself around its employees, and the result was several project teams. There were no organizational charts or job descriptions. A management committee made up of directors of functional areas takes all decisions relating to company strategy. A subcommittee proposes new projects and appoints project leaders; the project leader is then responsible for choosing his or her team from the available employees. The employees rotate between projects, and work on more than one project at a time. A computer-

Oticon's basic human values are embodied in the following assumptions	How do we put these assumptions into practice?
Oticon employees like to take responsibility if they are offered it	Wherever possible, and especially within the context of a given project, the employee chooses his own tasks and his hours and place of work
Oticon employees want to develop and grow in their jobs, and to meet new challenges within the company	We make it possible for an employee to work on several tasks at once, if he has the interest and the ability, with the support of colleagues if necessary
Oticon employees want as much freedom as possible, but they also accept the need for a clear and structured framework, mainly in the form of an accepted strategy and approved plans	Oticon has as few rules as possible; we encourage staff to use their common sense rather than becoming slaves to rules
Oticon employees want fair and competent feedback on their work, and they want their salary to reflect the contribution which they make to the company	Managers at all levels (technical, staff, project) should give their employees honest feedback, negative as well as positive. All employees have a yearly discussion with their mentors. To arrive at fair salary adjustments, Oticon takes into account assessments made by the employee's project and technical managers
Oticon employees want to be partners in the company, not its adversaries	From time to time employees have a chance to buy Oticon shares at a favourable rate; this allows them to benefit financially from the success to which they have contributed
Oticon employees want the security that comes from improving themselves in their current jobs, so that they will be able to get another one if they should leave Oticon for any reason	We enable staff to improve themselves in their jobs and to take on other tasks in the company wherever appropriate. We expect employees to show initiative and to be willing to make an effort, e.g. by taking courses in their spare time
Oticon employees want to be treated as independent adults	Oticon's whole manner of operating is based on this assumption
Oticon employees want to see how their own tasks fit into the workings of the whole company	Oticon is an open company in which all employees have access to as much information as possible. The limits are set partly by the law on data protection, and partly by the fact that certain pieces of information are so sensitive that we cannot risk their getting into the wrong hands. When Oticon is quoted on the Copenhagen Stock Exchange, we shall have to respect the stock exchange's code of conduct, which limits access to certain types of information
Oticon employees are more interested in having challenging tasks than in formal status and titles	We have a minimum number of titles and no formal career planning. However, we try to give each employee opportunities for personal and professional development, by providing varied tasks which present increasing levels of challenge

Figure 63 Oticon's Basic Values.

based information system keeps track of the projects and of the availability of employees for work of specific kinds. A project leader can scan the list of employees to find out who is available. Each employee defines his or her own job and joins projects needing those particular skills.

The unique quality of Oticon as a learning environment derives not only from the project-based form of organization but also from other supporting policies: the company has started to use open-plan offices, has stopped using paper, and has a new culture based on the Oticon Basic Values (Figure 63). In 1991, Oticon moved to a new location. Everyone now has a desk and a PC, but the desk can be put anywhere. It is stressed that everyone has to be able to move within five minutes.

There are no filing cabinets, just a pedestal containing essential information.

The CEO decided that paper would no longer be used. An IT system was designed for storing and retrieving documents. Today, all incoming mail is scanned and put into the system, then publicly shredded. This means that everyone can read the mail, because everyone has access to the system. All documented information can thus be shared. The system was designed to reduce paper work, support work processes and to encourage dialogue.

Thanks to project teams, open-plan offices, the elimination of paper, and the basic values, Oticon has become a learning organization. The company now intends to increase the efficiency of its communication, since this is also regarded as being essential to learning.

Case study 24

British Aerospace Plc

British Aerospace Plc is one of the UK's largest manufacturing companies. It is the biggest exporter of manufactured goods, selling more than 60 per cent of its products overseas. The group consists of a number of businesses: defence, commercial aircraft, Rover Group, Arlington Securities and Balast Nedham. The company's turnover in 1991 was £10,562 million: British Aerospace Defence Ltd contributed about 40 per cent of this, the Rover Group 35 per cent, and commercial aircraft about 16 per cent. At that time, the company employed about 120,000 people.

To enable the company to operate efficiently within a unified learning culture, the subsidiaries established an extensive and sophisticated employee development programme with several

on-the-job interventions. British Aerospace uses the term 'organization learning': this denotes the development of a learning culture aimed at improving business effectiveness. Three elements were considered necessary for building a learning organization: (1) a people strategy; (2) corporate learning days, and (3) priorities for learning.

People strategy

The people strategy states two objectives: to maximize the contribution made by individuals, and to use people to gain a competitive advantage for the business. The company plans to achieve its goals and fulfil its business plans by establishing appropriate organizational structures, finding the right people with the right skills, providing open communication channels and developing leaders. The cornerstones of this strategy are the creation of learning opportunities for all employees and the provision of an environment which gives individuals confidence, a sense of purpose and opportunities to achieve recognition no matter what their level in the organization. To create these conditions within the various businesses, the employee development group works with the subsidiaries (1) to ensure flat organizational structures; (2) to make sure that key positions are filled effectively; (3) to create development centres; (4) to foster employees with high potential; and (5) to establish an open working environment.

Corporate learning days
Corporate learning days have been held at the highest level to work on topics which the board identified as being critical to the business. These learning days are intended as an opportunity for sharing experience, arriving at an understanding of the company's strengths and weaknesses, and finding ways to overcome the weaknesses. The learning days featured interactive workshops, the purpose of which is to share knowledge, identify any gaps and

exploit opportunities. External input is obtained to avoid an insular approach.

Priorities for learning
Key performance indicators are identified by reference to the business plan, and an analysis was conducted of training needs. This yielded a list of core learning priorities. On the basis of these priorities, training programmes were refined, employees were rotated within the company, new channels of communication were established and a culture was created in which value was placed on learning. In addition, each business unit defined its own learning priorities, which are to be measured by means of key performance indicators. The intention was to propel each of the businesses into a new era.

These activities show how British Aerospace envisaged organizational learning. Human resource management has been selected as an important area for learning. Organizational learning has been brought about mainly by building a framework consisting of open communication, alignment of the goals of individuals with those of the organization, and continuous assessment of changing needs.

4 Maps

We live in a world composed of our ideas, knowledge, plans and images. These determine how we talk and think and how we present ourselves to others. They also determine which parts of reality we perceive as interesting and important. Many scientists have used the idea of a conceptual map as a metaphor for this representation of reality. A map is a web of interpretations formed from implicit interests and fears; it expresses the various aspects of our world and determines when action is necessary. It is a cognitive representation of the world and of the individual.

For managers, who have to cope with ambiguity, the visual development of maps is a useful way of representing mental processes. Just like the more traditional maps, mental maps are aids to making connections between

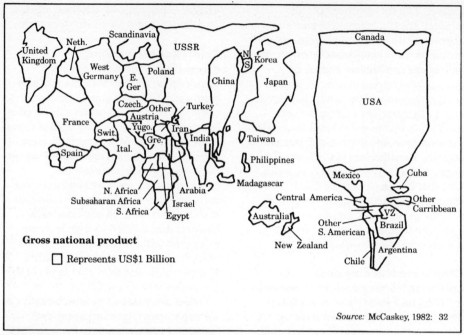

Gross national product

☐ Represents US$1 Billion

Source: McCaskey, 1982: 32

Figure 64 Map of world from the perspective of GNP.

assumptions and actions. The maps are not always correct, never complete, and are always in need of further revision (McCaskey, 1982).

Figure 64 shows how our imagination allows us to draw a map which emphasizes one aspect and thus distorts the complete picture. Maps can be revised; this makes mapping an important tool for coping with ambiguity, because new sections can be drawn into old maps or sections can be changed.

Organizations, groups and individuals use maps to create for themselves a picture of reality, which they use as a basis for action. In most cases, the maps are used in such a way that the existing picture of reality is confirmed. Argyris and Schön (1978) describe this as the self-sealing quality of maps. Elements which do not fit into the picture or which might cause anxiety are often ignored and cut out of the picture. Another reason why maps are difficult to change is that constructing them is a long and arduous process. The picture of reality has to be confirmed and verified by interaction with others. Letting go of a map is a 'little dying'. The need for stability which exists both in people and in systems is often underestimated. The desire to hold onto the past is completely understandable; the process of allowing one map to die so that a new one can be drawn costs a great effort and is associated with feelings of uncertainty and loss. The process must therefore be properly acknowledged.

There are several steps which need to be completed before a 'little dying' can be brought about, allowing new and different maps to be drawn. In times of crisis or conflict, or in problem situations, organizations seem to go through the following stages:

- *Shock*: employees become aware of the threat to existing structures
- *Defensive attitude*: old maps are retained and defended
- *Insight*: old maps are compared and questioned
- *Adaptation and change*: new maps and structures are formed, and the meaning behind them is reconstructed

These processes are prerequisites for learning in groups. Working in a group to analyze assumptions and to develop maps which integrate norms and values can create a basis for working together.

Example: Mapping

Mapping is an instrument for the visual representation of cognitive maps. It can be used with individuals or with groups. It offers a structured way of visualization. The available knowledge is classified and ordered both at the individual and organizational level. It is the interactive process of sharing content and revealing the underlying premises which leads to organizational learning. The process results in the formation of cognitive maps, which provide the framework for further action.

Before this new framework can be constructed, old cognitive maps must be questioned. Cognitive distortions strengthen existing mental models and thus hinder learning. Deliberate measures must be taken to overcome the consequences of these distortions. Figure 65 shows different kinds of distortion, their consequences and measures which can be taken to overcome them.

Case study 25

ABB Industrie Ltd

Mind-mapping is a way of making notes for planning and problem solving and for releasing creativity (Svantesson, 1992). Initial thought processes are chaotic and do not proceed in straight lines or along logical paths. Thoughts follow many directions at the same time. Mind-mapping is an attempt to produce a visual record of these thoughts, thus prompting creative processes. It is an instrument which combines imagination with structure, and pictures with logic (see the figures in this and the next case study).

In the initial, creative phase, a central concept is chosen and the subject writes down everything which he or she associates with it. Moving out from the centre, all the words are recorded, but without any structure. Once the ideas have been put on paper, a discussion is held with another person. In the course of this discussion, concepts are grouped, generic terms located and categories defined. These are emphasized by means of drawings, using colours. This creates a clear picture of the central concept. The result is a mind-map structured according to chosen criteria.

Cognitive distortion	Consequences	Corrective measures: 'analyze the context of your decision'
Availability	Probability of easily remembered events is overestimated	Do not ignore information because it is difficult to access
Selective perception	Expectations distort observation of strategy-relevant variables	Pay prompt attention to the seemingly unimportant variables as well as to the important ones
Illusory correlation	Confidence makes people believe that unconnected variables are correlated	Check the supposed correlations
Conservatism	Predictions based on new information are ignored	Revise your forecasts if indicated by new information
Law of small numbers	Too few examples are taken as representative of the larger population	Do not generalize from individual cases
Tendency towards the mean	Levelling of scattered data	Do not ignore the extremes
Wishful thinking	Probability of the desired event is greatly overestimated	Do not underestimate probability of undesired events
Delusions of power	Degree of personal control over the event is overestimated	Do not overestimate your sphere of influence
Logical reconstruction	'Logical' reconstruction of imperfectly remembered events	Do not attempt to reconstruct courses of events unless you know them better
Ability to predict	Predictability of earlier events is overestimated	Be realistic about your ability to predict
Availability	Use of the first analogy that comes to mind	Look carefully for the best analogy or metaphor
Failure to differentiate	Over-simplification as a result of using (1) an analogy which is too simple for a highly complex problem, or (2) a single analogy	Use more differentiated analogies or metaphors, or use several if necessary
Non-comparability	Denial of critical differences between existing situation and analogy employed	Pay attention to differences between the real situation and the analogy
Exclusiveness	Problems are defined and solved exclusively by use of the analogy, as a result of overestimation of problem-solving ability	Use analogies and metaphors for support only

Source: based on Naujoks, 1993, and Schwenk, 1988

Figure 65 Measures for avoiding typical errors in interpretation by individuals.

Mind-mapping is an instrument which helps to chart information (Buzan, 1993). Since the brain works primarily with key concepts, the drawings help to represent central ideas. The use of this method leads to the birth of new ideas and the solution of problems. It is a useful practical instrument because people can solve problems by sharing and comparing mind-maps. Individual cognitive patterns are revealed in the course of discussions, and this places them at the disposal of the organization. It is a useful instrument that promotes learning: the building of cognitive maps increases the number of problem-solving strategies in the organization's knowledge base. In ABB, this method has been used to chart the contexts in which human resource development takes place. It sets human resource development in the wider context of the learning organization (Figure 66).

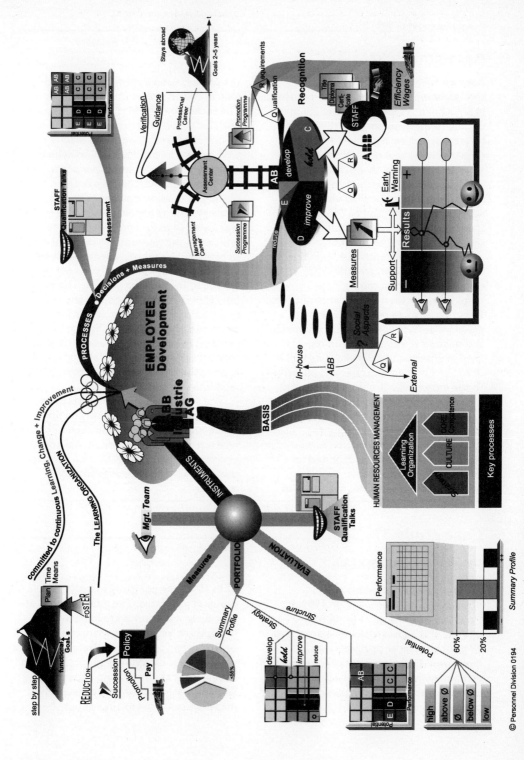

Figure 66 ABB's Human resource development mind map.

Case study 26

Aare-Emmenkanal Ltd

Aare-Emmenkanal (AEK) is an energy and telecommunications company based in Solothurn, Switzerland. The company wished to increase employees' awareness of internal objectives so that they would be able to adjust their actions accordingly. A workshop was therefore held to consolidate the company's strategy and its vision and mission statement, and to represent them visually. The method chosen was the mind-mapping technique.

The company wanted all members to feel part of the firm, whether they were employees of longstanding, new employees, or even potential employees. The company had realized that the problem did not lie in the current vision and mission statement, but in its implementation in daily working life. A vision and mission statement is effective to the extent that it unites the ideas of everyone in the system and is experienced as a living thing. AEK decided to use mind-mapping to facilitate the implementation of the vision and mission statement and to initiate a learning process.

Mind-mapping enables members of the organization to develop a mental map of the organization and its goals. The technique was first intended for use with individuals but was not applied in its original form: it was used mainly with groups to produce a chart which can be used for corrective purposes.

The groups charted the company's vision and mission statement and its strategy, taking a global view. The result was a shared map. The lively picture in which this is presented makes a lasting impression. However, the map can be discussed at any time, and changed or extended by working groups. The map only shows certain aspects of the organization. To make it easier for everyone to take part in the mapping process, the mind-map was distributed throughout the company for discussion. It was then reworked on the basis of the feedback (Figure 67).

The second map was thus based on the information contained in the first, plus additional information such as written and oral feedback. It was the process of working together to produce this map which led to organizational learning.

Case study 27

Hoffmann–La Roche

Hoffmann–La Roche is a Swiss pharmaceuticals company. In 1991, its total sales amounted to SF 11,451 million; this represented an increase of 18 per cent on the previous year. Hoffmann–La Roche is an international company operating in more than 100 countries, and employing over 5,000 people.

In 1992, the company identified a group of problems. The development of new drugs takes on average between five and ten years. Each year, Hoffmann–La Roche had to go through the procedure of obtaining approval for new drugs. Over the years, the Federal Drug Administration (FDA) has repeatedly made the same complaints about

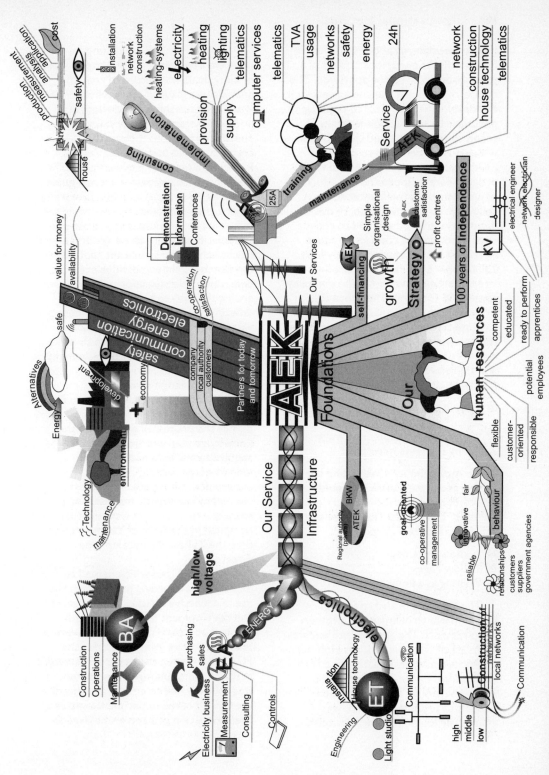

Figure 67 Adapted mind map after feedback process.

incomplete data, or about the need for further checks on various aspects of a product before it can be approved. The company therefore launched a research and development project to improve the processes by which knowledge is acquired and shared, and the ways in which it is applied so as to provide maximum leverage. The aims of this project were to speed the introduction of products onto the market by reducing the approval time, to avoid disapproval of products and to reduce costs. The average costs for product development are approximately US$ 250 million. Each day that a product is late onto the market costs the company about US$ 1 million. Therefore this project was of particular importance.

A specific objective was to avoid the tendency to repeat the same mistakes in reports prepared for the FDA. A project was therefore set up to answer the following questions:

■ Who in our company knows something about this problem?
■ Why are our customers always asking the same questions?

The company hoped that finding the answers to these questions would help it to overcome organizational barriers to learning. The project team developed three tools for this purpose:

■ A knowledge map
■ Yellow Pages
■ Writing as a knowledge tool

The first step in analyzing the problem was to define key customer requirements. The appropriate experts were asked what procedures Hoffmann–La Roche was using to satisfy the FDA regulations. Every step, from the basic research through the development process to product approval, was charted by looking at the relationships between the scientists working in different departments. The knowledge of individuals was recorded and an analysis was made of areas where there was a need for sharing knowledge.

The process of analysis was a time-consuming one, but it resulted in the creation of two useful tools: the knowledge map and Yellow Pages. The knowledge map provides a visual guide to the experience of individuals working on drug development. By recording the stages in the development process and the relationships involved, Hoffmann–La Roche achieved a significant reduction in development time. Individuals had to contribute relevant information to enable the map to be drawn, and differing approaches to development were recorded. Hoffmann–La Roche plans to computerize the map to make it available to new product development teams.

The knowledge map was supplemented by two other tools. The first of these was the Yellow Pages. As part of the process of developing the knowledge map and analyzing customer requirements, a list was made of individuals possessing relevant experience (Figure 68). This list of bearers of knowledge represented the store of expertise, and was eventually compiled in the form of Yellow Pages (like the Yellow Pages telephone directory).

The second tool which helped to expedite the approval process was the use of collective writing. The research and development teams which had worked on a particular product were asked to write a joint report for the FDA. This helped the teams to develop a shared understanding of the various stages. It also led to critical analysis of the quality of the experiments and to the production of a better message for

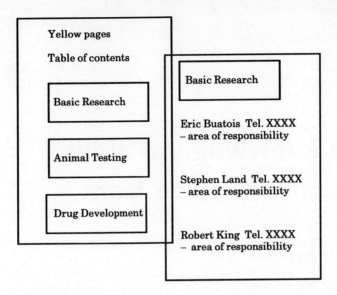

Figure 68 Yellow Pages.

the report. The process of joint writing was used as a tool to stimulate thinking and to facilitate communication beyond the limits of the document itself.

The use of the knowledge map and the supporting tools made the division into a learning organization: knowledge was shared across functional boundaries, existing organizational structures and habits were questioned, and new organizational systems were created. All of this supported the work involved in obtaining approval for a product. Product development times and costs were reduced, and the effectiveness of the division was increased.

12

From knowledge to ability to the intention to learn

Organizations are capable of learning; indeed, they must learn, because no-one knows what the future will bring. The need to learn is not in dispute. However, as we have seen, it is not easy to find a common element on which to base a simple definition of learning by organizations. Even more diverse are opinions on how organizational learning processes can best be influenced and channelled. However, this very diversity is a source of great potential. Companies can gain a great deal if they consider the different views on organizational learning in relation to their own difficulties.

1 Definitions of learning

The literature on organizational learning reveals uncertainty in explanation and gross differences between definitions (Garvin, 1993; Fiol and Lyles, 1985; Senge, 1990). There is general agreement on two points only: first, that the phenomenon does exist, and secondly, that organizations that do not learn cannot make progress because they keep on repeating existing behaviour patterns. These patterns fail to meet new challenges, so the company fails to develop.

Definitions of learning do not give satisfactory answers to questions such as: what difference does learning really make? What initiates it? How can it be measured? Can it be measured in terms of the tools for learning which a company may possess? Is it enough if the company shows suitable ways of thinking? Are observable changes in behaviour patterns required? It is not enough if an observer decides that the potential for change is there just because the company's instruments include suitable systems, instruments and ways of thinking. We need to be able to see how instruments are interpreted and used. We would therefore wish to define organizational learning as follows:

> **the ability of the institution as a whole to discover errors and correct them, and to change the organization's knowledge base and values so as to generate new problem-solving skills and new capacity for action.**

After reading through the majority of this book, one may ask about the difference between organizational learning and organizational development. Although both refer to improved behaviour by the organization, organizational development is the wider term. Organizational development does not specify the area of change whereas organizational learning refers specifically to a change in organizational knowledge and values.

2 Knowledge: instruments for learning

We need a definition of learning because without one we cannot tell whether a system has learned or not. The mere fact that a technique exists does not mean that it is being used. The concept of total quality management (TQM) is a case in point. It is often taken to mean increased employee participation in order to increase quality. Using TQM could in fact lead to organizational learning: but success does not depend on the knowledge about the instrument itself but its use within the organization.

The techniques that we have described for facilitating organizational learning must also be seen in relative terms. It was not our intention to describe these techniques in detail, and we have not attempted to produce a comprehensive list of aids to learning or breaking down barriers to learning. We believe that this would simply cause confusion. One and the same technique can facilitate or hinder learning: its effects depend on how it is interpreted and applied. In other words, the vital element is the *process*.

Management by objectives (MBO), for example, can be interpreted and used either as a direct, goal-specific and individual method, or it can be used as a group-based method involving interactions between members. If it is used as an individual method, it is likely to be a barrier to learning. Action is taken to meet objectives; there is no room for initiatives or consideration because they serve no purpose. Creativity and readiness to take risks are excluded; the attitude is often one of indifference or detachment. However, when MBO is used as a group method, views are exchanged, ideas are noticed and even rewarded, objectives are discussed and questioned, and a win–win approach is taken to the analysis of situations. When used in this way, MBO stimulates organizational learning processes.

We have outlined the various kinds of technique for promoting learning and given examples of ways in which learning processes can be initiated and supported. We chose examples from the fields of structure, strategy, culture and human resource management. It is important to know what methods are available; it is even more important to know *how* they should be used. We have therefore emphasized the processes involved in facilitating learning (Chapters 7–11). The different instruments for learning are important, yet they constitute only the minimum requirements for it. No matter how well instruments are chosen and applied, learning is not something that can be imposed.

3 Ability: can we make learning happen?

It should be clear by now that learning is not something that can be ordered, but that it is an outcome of processes. It arises from systems themselves and cannot be reduced to individual measures, methods, persons, etc. We do not believe that it is possible to impose a definitive structure either on learning by individuals or on learning by organizations. One cannot simply teach the system what to do, how to think or how to behave. Galileo wrote: 'One cannot teach a man anything. One can only help him to discover it within himself.' We believe this to be true of institutions too. Learning cannot be imposed; it emerges from the system itself.

Organizational learning involves the development of new behaviour patterns or new potential for problem-solving. It is not something which can be imposed upon the system. Conditions can be created which facilitate learning processes, permit certain directions to be taken, and strengthen feedback. However, the system is a self-organizing entity, and it is always the system which acts, chooses and decides.

This brings us to the essential point. When we reach the limits of what can be done, the next step should not be to give up but to develop a *process orientation*. We must create conditions which trigger learning processes, permit them to develop, and channel and support them. These learning processes can take place in the areas we have already mentioned — development of strategy, structure, culture and human resources. In addition to knowing what methods can be useful and meaningful in these areas, it is important to be able to apply them so that they facilitate learning, and take advantage of opportunities for learning. It is important to recognize what can be done to bring about learning, what potentials can be realized, and when and how learning can be directed within existing structures. Organizational members must also be provided with the necessary conditions for learning. These include opportunities for communication, interaction and analysis, and the creation of transparency. Communication is the process in which participants use a common language to talk about different views and interpretations of reality, and make them transparent and accessible to others. This creates the shared frame of reference within which learning processes can take place.

4 Intention: the will to learn

There is a third factor upon which organizational learning depends, and to which we have paid little attention in this book. Without it learning cannot take place and behaviour will not change. We have already said that learning cannot be made to happen but that it must proceed from the system itself. If a person or a whole organization does not want to learn, it will not do so. It is the learning organization itself which decides whether it is willing to learn. People and organizations must be *ready and willing* to question expectations, values, experiences and actions. They must be willing to change and be prepared to steer their expectations etc. into new and unknown paths.

Organizational learning in social systems is a product not only of knowledge about instruments and ability but also of the willingness for change. This means that the company must be ready to broaden and enrich its internal potential, and to order its activities in a meaningful way, keeping in mind its ethical principles.

5 Maturity of the organization

The actual choice of methods depends very much on the maturity of the organization. Internal and external consultants who want to initiate organizational learning processes must start from where the organization actually is. They need to determine the level of maturity of the organization for two main reasons: first, it will help them to identify possible approaches, and secondly, they will be in a better position to assess potential for conflict.

It may not be easy to evaluate the level of maturity of a company, but it ought to be done. The level at which an organization is able to learn is a relative rather than an absolute quality, and depends on the maturity of the organization. Organizational learning implies a qualitative change in the frame of reference which itself changes over time. If the level of maturity of the company is wrongly assessed then the system may be either overchallenged or under-challenged. If the system is overchallenged, the measures adopted will not be taken up by the members of the organization because they will either fail to understand them or will see them as meaningless. Discussions in which people are encouraged to speak out may overchallenge companies which have a bureaucratic tradition because the employees have no experience of participation and have not learned to argue in such situations. If, on the other hand, the participants in the learning process are not given enough opportunity to become involved and use their potential, the measures adopted may be underchallenging the system.

If we wish to institute a learning process in our company, and need, therefore, to assess its level of maturity for organizational learning, we must use all of the three criteria just described: knowledge, ability and intention (Figure 69). This gives us a three-dimensional description of its status. The dimensions may be defined as follows:

■ Knowledge: the number of learning instruments
■ Ability: the learning level
■ Intention: the willingness to learn

It will be apparent from these definitions that the level of maturity cannot be measured in simple quantitative terms. The number of learning instruments, the ability to learn and the readiness to learn depend on the stage of development of the organization and cannot be objectively determined.

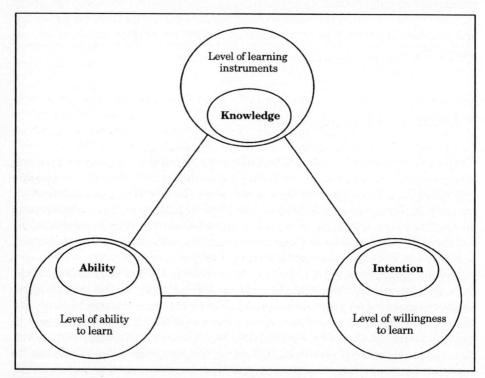

Figure 69 Maturity factors in organizational learning.

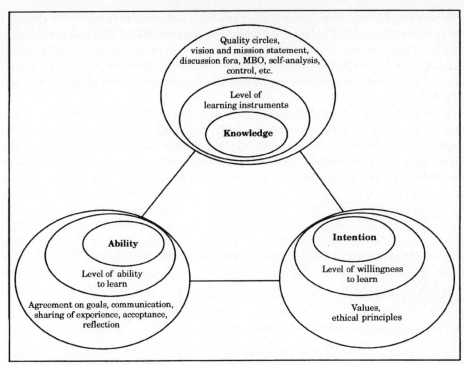

Figure 70 Interplay of knowledge, ability and intention.

Assessment of the level of maturity also depends on the observer's interpretation and is therefore subjective. This level cannot, therefore, be determined with scientific exactitude. We now look at various questions which may be asked in relation to each of the three dimensions (Figure 70).

The first question is, what *instruments* are available to support learning processes? Is there a vision and mission statement, so that the company's attitudes to productivity, finances, employees, etc. can be examined? Is there an information system, which gives the signals needed for an early warning system? Is there a formal or informal network for sharing problem-solving strategies? Does the organization contain development alliances which facilitate analysis of values and acceptance of differences?

Organizational learning will only happen if there is the *ability* to make appropriate use of the available instruments. The presence of an instrument is in itself no guarantee. The organization must be able to discuss conflicting aims, accept criticism in feedback discussions and negotiate. It must also be able to carry out critical analyses of goal fulfilment, disclose the results and discuss them in group settings. Individual employees and groups must be trained to analyze situations, point out strengths and weaknesses, list and evaluate possible solutions in a creative way, and question their own actions.

Finally, individuals or groups must have the *intention* to learn. Why should I try to make changes? Why should I accept or support them? Do I see the point in this learning process? Do we have a shared frame of reference which will permit us to accept and examine different views, exchange opinions and trust others? When our values are involved, and when we can make sense of change, we want to learn.

It will now be clear that these three factors are the main determinants of the company's level of maturity with regard to learning. To determine the level of maturity from the point of view of knowledge, we need to look at the instruments and techniques which are present within the organization. These include all forms of intervention which can be instrumental in bringing about organizational learning, e.g. vision and mission statements, guidelines, job rotation, project work. These will generally be methods which strengthen the potential for self-development within a social system. We should remember that it is not only the number of instruments and techniques which is significant but also whether their implementation is process-based. We suggest the following three criteria for determining knowledge:

- Number of techniques for facilitating learning
- Number of techniques for breaking down barriers to learning
- Process-oriented use of techniques

Analyzing the knowledge factor does not give sufficient information for us to assess the level of maturity for learning. We must also consider whether the organization has the *ability* to make proper use of the available techniques. The presence in the company of the following may be used as assessment criteria:

- Ability to cooperate and participate
- Ability to communicate and achieve transparency
- Ability to analyze problems and solve complex issues
- Ability to store knowledge

The final stage in assessing the level of maturity to learn is to analyze the motivation. The question here is whether the organization is interested in learning. To answer it, we need to ask whether the company

- Creates a structure which imparts meaning
- Builds on an ethical basis
- Wants to create a shared value system

The organization's readiness to learn may then be shown as in Figure 71.

We have seen that to assess an organization's readiness to learn, we need to look at instruments, its ability and its intention. Once we have done this, and we know where to start, how is learning to be brought about? How can we approach the various fields of learning? How can we guide learning processes so as to achieve a new order which can accommodate new behaviours?

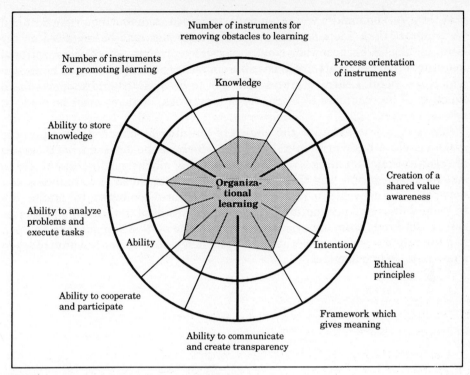

Figure 71 Maturity of learning organization.

Order in social systems can arise in many ways. A particular order consists in the continual interchange of theories of action which are shared by individual and groups within a company. New patterns can arise from very different starting points. Learning processes can therefore have the same outcome in companies of different kinds. Conversely, similar companies can produce very different results. The important factors are how the learning techniques are applied, what use is made of abilities and how the will to learn is expressed.

6 The building block principle

If we want to help a social system to achieve a new level of learning, we need to start at several points at once. We must analyze and make changes in several areas at the same time, i.e. in structure, culture, strategy and human resources. We need to know where we want to go and what abilities are needed, and make sure that we possess the necessary instruments in the right combination. Instruments and abilities must be put together like a child's building blocks so that they *fit*. The factors which we have described as favouring organizational learning are thus 'tools for learning'. The examples may be regarded as the building blocks, because they contain possible cornerstones of organizational learning. From the repertoire of possible courses of action, blocks can be chosen which are useful. Learning processes ought to be initiated and supported as a function of its readiness to learn. As in a network, changes must be made at several points.

The design principle, i.e. the choice of building blocks, depends upon the system itself. A basic principle — and one which can be derived from the goals of organizational learning — is that the building blocks may be used freely to suit the organization, and that they should be combined so as to function as a network and generate meaning. Instruments are combined to create the necessary links and interactions. However, the result of the learning processes can proceed only from the system itself. Only the system can act, can be open and tolerant towards new methods and decide whether or not it wants to learn a new pattern of behaviour.

Bibliography

Argyris, C. (1985) *Strategy, Change and Defensive Routines*, Pitman, Massachusetts.

Argyris, C. (1990) *Overcoming Organizational Defenses: Facilitating Organizational Learning*, Allyn & Bacon, Boston.

Argyris, C. and Schön, D.A. (1978) *Organizational Learning: A Theory of Action Perspective*, Addison-Wesley, Reading, Mass.

Bandura, A. (1979) *Sozial-kognitive Lerntheorie*, Stuttgart.

Bateson, G. (1981) *Ökologie des Geistes*, Suhrkamp, Frankfurt.

Berger, P. and Luckmann, T. (1990) *Die gesellschaftliche Konstruktion der Wirklichkeit: Eine Theorie der Wissensoziologie*, Suhrkamp, Frankfurt.

Bloch, P., Hababou, R. and Xarde, D. (1986) *Service compris*, L'expansion, Hachette/Jean-Claude Lattès, Paris.

Borer, C. and Broggi, M. (1991) 'Unternehmensleitbild mit Mindmapping', *IO Management Zeitschrift*, **6**: 27–30.

Bower, G. and Hilgard, E. (1983) *Theorie des Lernens I*, Poeschel, Stuttgart.

Burke (1992) *Organization Development: A Process of Learning and Changing*, Addison-Wesley, Reading, Mass.

Buzan, T. (1993) *Kopftraining: Anleitung zum kreativen Denken*, Goldmann, Munich.

Cangelosi, V. and Dill, W. (1965) 'Organizational learning: observations toward a theory', *Administrative Science Quarterly*, **10**, 175–203.

Cohen, W. and Levinthal, D. (1990) 'Absorptive capacity: a new perspective on learning and innovation', *Administrative Science Quarterly*, **28**: 223–44.

Cyert, R. and March, J. (1963) *A Behavioral Theory of the Firm*, Prentice Hall, Englewood Cliffs, NJ.

De Geus, A. (1988) 'Planning as learning', *Harvard Business Review*, **66**: 70–4.

Deiss, G. and Dierolf, K. (1991) 'Strategische Planung und Frühwarnung durch Netzwerke', in Probst and Gomez (eds), *Vernetztes Denken, op. cit.*, pp. 211–26.

Dörner, D. (1987) Memorandum No. 54, Bamberg, Working Paper.

Dörner, D. (1989) *Die Logik des Misslingens: Strategisches Denken in komplexen Situationen*, Rowohlt, Hamburg.

Drucker, P. (1980) *Managing in Turbulent Times*, Harper & Row, New York.

Duncan, R. and Weiss, A. (1979) 'Organizational learning: implications for organizational design', *Research in Organizational Behavior*, **1**: 75–123.

Escher, F. (1993) 'Notizen aus der Schule der Komplexität', in *Managerie 2: Jahrbuch für systemisches Management*, Karl Auer Verlag, Heidelberg.

Esser, J., Lindoerfer, J. K. and Joanne, S. (1989) 'Groupthink and the space shuttle Challenger accident: toward a quantitative case analysis', *Journal of Behavioral Decision Making*, **2**: 245–78.

Fankhauser, P. and Probst, G. (1993) 'Die strategische Einheit "Geschäftsreisen"', in Gomez and Probst (eds), *Handbuch zur genzheitlichen strategischen Führung, op. cit.*

Fiol, C. (1994) 'Consensus, diversity, and learning in organizations', *Organization Science*, **5**: 403–20.

Fiol, C. and Lyles, M. (1985) 'Organizational learning', *Academy of Management Review*, **10**: 803–13.

Fuchs, J. (1990) 'Die Dienstleistungspyramide im Unternehmen', in Little, A. (ed.), *Management der Hochleistungsorganisation*, Gabler, Wiesbaden, pp. 137–47.

Garratt, B. (1990) *Creating a Learning Organization: A Guide to Leadership*, Learning and Development, Cambridge.

Garratt, B. (1995) *Learning to Lead: Developing your Organization and Yourself*, Harper Collins, Glasgow.

Garvin, D. (1993) 'Building a learning organization', *Harvard Business Review*, July/Aug., 78–91.

Geißler, H. (1991) 'Organisations-Lernen: Gebot und Chance einer zukunftsweisenden Pädagogik', *Grundlagen der Weiterbildung Zeitschrift*, **1**: 72–9.

Gomez, P. and Probst, G. (1993) *Handbuch zur ganzheitlichen strategischen Führung*, Schweizerische Kurse für Unternehmensführung, Zurich.

Hammer, M. and Champy, J. (1993) *Reengineering the Corporation: A Manifesto for Business Revolution*, Harper Business, New York.

Harris, P. (1985) *Management in Transition*, Jossey-Bass, San Francisco.

Hedberg, B. (1981) 'How organizations learn and unlearn', in Nystrom, P.C. and Starbuck, W.H. (eds), *Handbook of Organizational Design*, London, pp. 8–27.

Hedlund, G. (1986) 'The hypermodern MNC — a heterarchy?' *Human Resource Management*, **25**: 9–35.

Hoffmann, V. (1993) 'Unternehmen als lernfähige Denkfabriken im Praxistest: Lernen in und mit Szenarien', in *Gabler's Magazin*, Sonderdruck Nr. 10, Gabler, Wiesbaden, pp. 25–28.

Hörrmann, G. and Tiby, C. (1990) 'Projektmanagement richtig gemacht', in Little, A. (ed.), *Management der Hochleistungsorganisation*, Gabler, Wiesbaden, pp. 73–91.

Hof, v., G. (1991) 'Vernetztes Denken und Handeln bei der Führung von Arbeitsgruppen und eines Projektes — Dargestellt an Beispielen aus der Allianz Versicherung', in Probst and Gomez (eds.), *Vernetztes Denken, op. cit.*, pp. 249–73.

Huber, G. (1991) 'Organizational learning: the contributing processes and the literatures', *Organization Science*, **2**(1): 88–115.

IBM Transformator (1993) *Das einmalige Magazin der neuen IBM*, Zurich.

Iikubo, H. (1990) 'Innovation in Japan am Beispiel Honda', *Bulletin der SKA* (Schweizerische Kreditanstalt), Zurich, 2/90: 12–13.

Janis, I. (1972) *Victims of Groupthink*, Houghton Mifflin, Boston.

Jelinek, M. (1979) *Institutionalizing Innovation: A Study of Organizational Learning*, Basil Blackwell, New York.

Kanter, R.M. (1983) *The Change Master: Innovation and Entrepreneurship in the American Corporation*, Simon & Schuster, New York.

Kasper, H. (1990) *Die Handhabung des Neuen in organisierten Sozialsystemen*, Springer, Berlin.

Kelly, G. (1955) *The Psychology of Personal Constructs*, Norton, New York.

Kilmann, R. (1984) *Beyond the Quick Fix*, Jossey-Bass, San Francisco.

Klimecki, R. and Probst, G. (1990) 'Entstehung und Entwicklung der Unternehmens-kultur', in Lattmann, C. (ed.), *Unternehmenskultur*, Physika, Heidelberg, pp. 41–65.

Klimecki, R., Probst, G. and Eberl, P. (1991) 'Systementwicklung als Management problem', in Staehle, W. and Sydow, J. (eds.), *Managementforschung 1*, Walter de Gruyter, Berlin/New York, pp. 103–62.

Klimecki, R., Probst, G. and Eberl, P. (1994) *Entwicklungsorientiertes Management*, Poeschel, Stuttgart.

Lawler III, E. (1992) *The Ultimate Advantage: Creating the High-involvement Organization*, Jossey-Bass, San Francisco.

Lessing, R. (1991) 'Strategische Planung als Lernprozeß — "Von mir aus nennt es Körper, Geist und Seele" ', in Sattelberger (ed.), *Die lernende Organisation, op. cit.*, pp. 261–72.

Levitt, B. and March, J.B. (1988) 'Organizational learning', *Annual Review of Sociology*, **14**: 319–40.

Lewin, K. (1951) *Field Theory in Social Science*, Wiley, New York.

Lorange, P. and Roos, J. (1992) *Strategic Alliances: Formation, Implementation and Evolution*, Blackwell Business, Massachusetts.

Love, J. (1988) *McDonalds: Behind the Arches*, Bantam, Toronto.

Lutz, C. (1991) 'Kommunikation — Kern der Selbstorganisation: Unternehmensführung im Informationszeitalter', in Sattelberger (ed.), *Die lernende Organisation, op. cit.*, pp. 97–109.

Magyar, K. and Prange, P. (1993) *Zukunft im Kopf–Wege zum Visionären Unternehmen*, Haufer, Freiburg.

March, J. and Olsen, J. (1976) 'Organizational learning and the ambiguity of the past', in *Ambiguity and Choice of Organizations*, Bergen, pp. 54–67.

March, J. and Simon, H. (1958) *Organizations*, Wiley, New York.

Maturana, A. (1982) 'Reflexionen: Lernen oder ontogenetischer Drift', *Delfin II*, December, 60–71.

McCaskey, M. (1982) *The Executive Challenge: Managing Change and Ambiguity*, Pitman, Boston.

Meadows, D., Meadows, D. and Randers, J. (1992) *Die neuen Grenzen des Wachstums*, DVA, Stuttgart.

Megginson, D. (1988) 'Instructor, coach, mentor: three ways of helping for managers', *Management Education and Development*, **19**(1): 198-210.

Morgan, G. (1986) *Images of Organization*, Sage, Newbury Park/London.

Nadler, D. and Tushman, M. (1977) 'A diagnostic model for organization behavior', in Hackman, J., Lawler, E. and Porter, W. (eds), *Perspectives on Behavior in Organizations*, McGraw-Hill, New York.

Naujoks, H. (1993) 'Autonomie in Organisationen: Perspektive und Handlungsleitlinie des Managements', Dissertation, St. Gallen.

Neuberger, O. (1991) *Personalentwicklung*, Ferdinand Enke Verlag, Stuttgart.

Nystrom, P. and Starbuck, W. (1984) 'Managing beliefs in organizations', *Journal of Applied Behavioral Science*, **20**: 277–87.

Ouchi, W. (1981) *Theory Z*, Addison-Wesley, Reading, Mass.

Pautzke, G. (1989) *Die Evolution der organisatorischen Wissensbasis: Bausteine zu einer Theorie des organisatorischen Lernens*, Verlag Barbara Kirsch, Herrsching.

Pawlowsky, P. (1992) 'Betriebliche Qualifikationsstrategien und organisationales Lernen', in Staehle, W.H. and Conrad, P. (eds.), *Managementforschung 2*, Walter de Gruyter, Berlin, pp. 177–237.

Peccei, A. (1979) *Zukunftschance Lernen*, Club of Rome Bericht über die 80er Jahre, Goldmann, Vienna.

Postman, L. and Underwood, B. (1973) 'Critical issues in interference theory', *Memory and Cognition*, **1**: 19–40.

Prange, C. (1996) 'Organizational learning', paper presented at Symposium on Organizational Learning and the Learning Organization at the Management School of Lancaster, 3–9 September 1996.

Probst, G. (1987) *Selbstorganisation*, Parey, Berlin.

Probst, G. (1989) 'So haben wir ein Leitbild eingeführt', *IO Management Zeitschrift*, **10**: 36–41.

Probst, G. (1993) *Organisation: Strukturen, Lenkungsinstrumente, Entwicklungsperspektiven*, Moderne Industrie, Lech.

Probst, G. and Gomez, P. (1991) *Vernetztes Denken: Unternehmen ganzheitlich führen*, Gabler, Wiesbaden.

Pümpin, C. and Geilinger, U. (1988) 'Strategische Führung', *Die Orientierung*, no. **76**: SVB, Bern.

Quinn-Mills, D. (1993) *Rebirth of the Corporation*, Wiley, New York.

Rühle, E. and Sauter-Sachs, S. (1992) *Strukturmanagement in schweizerischen Industrieunternehmungen*, Haupt, Bern.

Sackmann, S. (1991) *Cultural Knowledge in Organizations: Exploring the Collective Mind*, Sage, Newbury Park.

Sackmann, S. (1992) 'Culture and subcultures: an analysis of organizational knowledge', *Administrative Science Quarterly*, **37**(1): 140–61.

Sattelberger, T., ed. (1991a) *Die lernende Organisation*, Gabler, Wiesbaden.

Sattelberger, T. (1991b) 'Personalentwicklung neuer Qualität durch Renaissance helfender Beziehungen', in Sattelberger (ed.), *Die lernende Organisation, op. cit.*, pp. 207–27.

Sattelberger, T. (1991c) 'Die lerndende Organisation im magischen Dreieck von Strategie-, Kultur- und Strukturentwicklung', *Personalführung*, **4**: 286–95.

Schmidt, S. (1991) *Der Diskurs des Radikalen Konstruktivismus*, Suhrkamp, Frankfurt.

Schwenk, C. (1988) 'The cognitive perspective on strategic decision making', *Journal of Management Studies*, **25**(1): 41–55.

Senge, P. (1990a) *The Fifth Discipline: The Art and Practice of the Learning Organization*, Doubleday, New York.

Senge, P. (1990b) 'The leader's new work: building learning organizations', *Sloan Management Review*, Fall, 7–23.

Senge, P. and Sterman, J. (1992) 'Systems thinking and organizational learning: acting locally and thinking globally in the organization of the future', in Kochan, T. and Useem, M. (eds), *Transforming Organizations*, Oxford University Press, New York, pp. 353–70.

Shrivastava, P. (1983) 'Typology of organizational learning systems', *Journal of Management Studies*, **20**(1): 7–28.

Simon, H. (1991) 'Bounded rationality and organizational learning', *Organization Science*, **2**: 125–40.

Sommerlatte, T. and Wedekind, E. (1990) 'Leistungsprozesse und Organisationsstruktur', in Little, A. (ed.) *Hochleistungsorganisation*, Gabler, Wiesbaden, pp. 23–42.

Staehle, W. (1991) 'Redundanz, Slack und lose Kopplung in Organisationen: Eine Verschwendung von Ressourcen', in Staehle, W. and Sydow, J. (eds), *Managementforschung 1*, Walter de Gruyter, Berlin, pp. 313–45.

Svantesson, I. (1992) *Mind Mapping und Gedächtnistraining*, PLS Verlag, Bremen.

Sydow, J. (1992) *Is the Single Firm Vanishing? Inter-enterprise Networks, Labour and Labour Institutions*, Forum Series on Labour in a Changing World Economy, International Institute for Labour Studies, Geneva, pp. 34–65.

Taylor, W. (1991) 'The logic of global business: an interview with ABB's Percy Barnevik', *Harvard Business Review*, March/April, 91–105.

Tichy, N. (1983) *Managing Strategic Change: Technical, Political, and Cultural Dynamics*, Wiley, New York.

Türk, K. (1989) *Neuere Entwicklungen in der Organisationsforschung: Ein Trend Report*, Ferdinand Enke Verlag, Stuttgart.

Ulrich, H. and Probst, G. (1988) *Anleitung zum ganzheitlichen Denken und Handeln: Ein Brevier für Führungskräfte*, Haupt, Bern.

Walsh, J. (1995) 'Managerial and organizational cognition: notes from a trip down memory lane', *Organization Science*, **6**: 280–321.

Walsh, J. and Ungson, G. (1991) 'Organizational memory', *Academy of Management Review*, **16**(1): 57–91.

Watzlawick, P. (1988) *Die erfundene Wirklichkeit*, Piper, Munich.

Watzlawick, P, Weakland, J. and Fisch, R. (1974) *Change*, Norton, New York.

Weick, K. and Bougon, M. (1986) 'Organizations as cognitive maps: Charting ways to success and failure', in Sims, Gioia *et al.* (eds), *The Thinking Organization: Dynamics of Organizational Social Cognition*, Jossey-Bass, San Francisco, pp. 102–35.

Weisbord, M. (1976) 'Organization diagnosis: six places to look for trouble with or without a theory', *Group and Organization Studies*, **1**: 430–47.

Whyte, G. (1989) 'Groupthink reconsidered', *Academy of Management Review*, **14**: 40–56.

Willke, H. (1991) *Systemtheorie*, UTB, Stuttgart.

World Competitiveness Report (1992) IMD, Lausanne.

Further reading

Adler, P. and Clark, K. (1991) 'Behind the learning curve: a sketch of the learning process', *Management Science*, **37**: 267–81.

Ansoff, H. (1977) 'Strategy formulation as a learning process: an applied managerial theory of strategic behavior', *International Studies of Management and Organization*, **7**, 58–77.

Argyris, C. (1983) *Reasoning, Learning and Action: Individual and Organizational*, Jossey-Bass, San Francisco.

Argyris, C. (1993) *On Organizational Learning*, Blackwell, Oxford.

Argyris, C. (1993) 'Education for leading-learning', *Organizational Dynamics*, **21**(3): 5–17.

Argyris, C. (1994) 'Good communication that blocks learning', *Harvard Business Review*, **72**: 77–85.

Belasco, J. (1990) *Teaching the Elephant to Dance: Empowering Change into Your Organization*, Century Business, London.

Bergquist, W. (1993) *The Post-modern Organization: Mastering the Art of Irreversible Change*, Jossey-Bass, San Francisco.

Boisot, M. (1995) 'Is your firm a creative destroyer? Competitive learning and knowledge flows in the technological strategies of firms', *Research Policy*, **24**: 489–506.

Bolmann, L. and Deal, T. (1991) *Reframing Organizations*, Jossey-Bass, San Francisco.

Bouwen, R. and Fry, R. (1991) 'Organizational innovation and learning: four patterns of dialog between the dominant logic and the new logic', *International Studies of Management and Organization*, **21**: 37–51.

Brooks, A. (1994) 'Power and the production of knowledge: collective team learning in work organizations', *Human Resource Development Quarterly*, **5**: 213–35.

Brown, J. and Duguid, P. (1991) 'Organizational learning and communities-of-practice: toward a unified view of working, learning and innovation', *Organization Science*, **2**: 40–57.

Bunning, C. (1992) 'Turning experience into learning: the strategic challenge for individuals and organizations', *Journal of European Industrial Training*, **16**: 7–12.

Burgelman, R. (1988) 'Strategy making as a social learning process: the case of internal corporate venturing', *Interfaces*, **18**: 74–85.

Burgoyne, J. (1992) 'Creating a learning organisation', *RSA Journal*, April, 1–10.

Burgoyne, J. (1994) 'Management by learning', *Management Learning*, **25**(1): 35–55.

Cohen, M. (1991) 'Individual learning and organizational routine: emerging connections', *Organization Science*, **2**: 135–9.

Cohen, W. and Levinthal, D. (1989) 'Innovation and learning: the two faces of R&D', *Economic Journal*, **99**: 569–96.

Coleman, W. (1994) 'Knowledge for action: a guide to overcoming barriers to organizational change', *Personnel Psychology*, **47**: 193–5.

Cook, S. and Yanow, D. (1993) 'Culture and organizational learning', *Journal of Management Inquiry*, **2**: 373–90.

Dixon, N. (1992) 'Organizational learning: a review of the literature with implications for HRD professionals', *Human Resource Development Quarterly*, **3**(1): 29–49.

Dodgson, M. (1991) *The Management of Technological Learning: Lessons from a Biotechnology Company*, de Gruyter, Berlin.

Dodgson, M. (1993) 'Organizational learning: a review of some literatures', *Organization Studies*, **14**: 375–94.

Dumaine, B. (1994) 'Mr. Learning Organization', *Fortune*, **130**: 147–57.

Epple, D., Argote, L. and Devadas, R. (1991) 'Organizational learning curves: a method for investigating intra-plant transfer of knowledge acquired through learning by doing', *Organization Science*, **2**(1): 58–71.

Etheredge, L.S. and Short, J. (1983) 'Thinking about government learning', *Journal of Mangement Studies*, **20**(1): 41–58.

Fox, S. (1994) 'Debating management learning', *Management Learning*, **25**(1): 83–93.

Fulmer, R. (1993) 'The tools of anticipatory learning', *Journal of Management Development*, **12**: 7–14.

Galer, G. and Van der Heijden, K. (1992) 'The learning organization: how planners create organizational learning', *Marketing Intelligence and Planning*, **10**: 5–12.

Geißler, H. (1992) 'Vom Lernen in der Organisation zum Lernen der Organisation', in Sattelberger, T. (ed.), *Die lernende Organisation*, Gabler, Wiesbaden, pp. 81–96.

Glynn, M-A. (1988) *Organizational Learning, Insight and Play*, Working Paper, Yale University, New Haven, Conn.

Haccoun, R. and Hamtiaux, T. (1994) 'Optimizing knowledge tests for inferring learning acquisition levels in single group training evaluation designs: the internal referencing strategy', *Personnel Psychology*, **47**: 593–604.

Hamel, G. (1991) 'Competition for competence and inter-partner learning within international strategic alliances', *Strategic Management Journal*, **12**: 83–103.

Hauser, E. (1988) 'Lernen: eine strategische Aufgabe im Unternehmen', *Management Zeitschrift*, **57**(10): 460–2.

Heidack, C. (1989) *Lernen der Zukunft*, Lexika, Munich.

Henry, J. and Walker, D. (1991) *Managing Innovation*, Sage, London.

Howard, R. (1990) *The Learning Imperative: Managing People for Continuous Innovation*, Harvard Business School, Boston, Mass.

Hutchins, E. (1991) 'Organizing work by adaptation', *Organization Science*, **2**(1): 14–39.

Inkpen, A. (1995) 'Believing is seeing: joint ventures and organization learning', *Journal of Management Studies*, **32**: 595–618.

182 Further reading

Isaacs, W. (1993) 'Dialogue, collective thinking, and organizational learning', *Organizational Dynamics*, Winter, 24–39.

Isaacs, W. and Senge, P. (1992) 'Overcoming limits to learning in computer-based learning environments', *European Journal of Operational Research*, **59**: 183–96.

Jones, A. and Hendry, C. (1994) 'The learning organization: adult learning and organizational transformation', *British Journal of Management*, **5**: 153–62.

Kiernan, M. (1993) 'The new strategic architecture: learning to compete in the twenty-first century', *Academy of Management Executive*, **7**: 7–21.

Kim, D. (1993) 'The link between individual and organizational learning', *Sloan Management Review*, **35**: 37–50.

Kochan, T.A. and Useem, M. (1992) *Transforming Organizations*, Oxford University Press, New York.

Kofman, F. and Senge, P. (1993) 'Communities of commitment: the heart of learning organizations', *Organizational Dynamics*, **22**: 5–23.

Lant, T. and Mezias, S. (1992) 'An organizational learning model of convergence and reorientation', *Organization Science*, **3**: 47–71.

Lant, T., Milliken, F. and Batra, B. (1992) 'The role of managerial learning and interpretation in strategic persistence and reorientation: an empirical exploration', *Strategic Management Journal*, **13**: 585–608.

Lawler, E. (1987) 'Changing organizations: strategic choices', Working Paper no. 106, University of Southern California.

Leonard-Barton, D. (1992) 'The factory as a learning laboratory', *Sloan Management Review*, **34**: 23–38.

Lessem, R. (1993) *Total Quality Learning*, Blackwell, Oxford.

Levinthal, D.A. (1991) 'Organizational adaptation and environmental selection: interrelated processes of change', *Organization Science*, **2**(1): 140–6.

Levinthal, D. and March, J. (1993) 'The myopia of learning', *Strategic Management Journal*, **14**: 95–112.

Lieberman, M. (1987) 'The learning curve, diffusion, and competitive strategy', *Strategic Management Journal*, **8**: 441–52.

Macdonald, S. (1995) 'Learning to change: an information perspective on learning in the organization', *Organization Science*, **6**: 557–68.

March, J., Sproull, L. and Tamuz, M. (1991) 'Learning from samples of one or fewer', *Organization Science*, **2**: 3–13.

McGill, M. and Slocum, J. (1993) 'Unlearning the organization', *Organizational Dynamics*, **22**: 67–79.

McGill, M., Slocum, Jr, J. and Lei, D. (1992) 'Management practices in learning organizations', *Organizational Dynamics*, **21**: 5–17.

Mills, D. and Friesen, B. (1992) 'The learning organization', *European Management Journal*, **10**: 146–56.

Mody, A. (1993) 'Learning through alliances', *Journal of Economic Behavior and Organization*, **20**: 151–70.

Morecroft, J. (1992) 'Executive knowledge, models and learning', *European Journal of Operational Research*, **59**: 9–27.

Mullen, T. and Lyles, M. (1993) 'Toward improving management development's contribution to organizational learning', *Human Resource Planning*, **16**: 35–49.

Nass, C. (1994) 'Knowledge or skills: which do administrators learn from experience?' *Organization Science*, **5**: 38–50.

Nevis, E., DiBella, A. and Gould, J. (1995) 'Understanding organizations as learning systems', *Sloan Management Review*, Winter, 73–85.

Nicolini, D. and Meznar, M. (1995) 'The social construction of organizational learning: conceptual and practical issues in the field', *Human Relations*, 48: 727–46.

Normann, R. (1985) 'Developing capabilities for organizational learning', in Pennings, J.M. *et al.* (eds), *Organizational Strategy and Change*, Jossey-Bass, San Francisco, pp. 217–48.

Nystrom, P. and Starbuck, W. (1984) 'To avoid organizational crises, Unlearn', *Organizational Dynamics*, Spring, 53–65.

Parkhe, A. (1991) 'Interfirm diversity, organizational learning, and longevity in global strategic alliances', *Journal of International Business Studies*, 22: 579–601.

Pennings, J., Barkema, H. and Douma, S. (1994) 'Organizational learning and diversification', *Academy of Management Journal*, 37: 608–40.

Pisano, G. (1994) 'Knowledge, integration, and the locus of learning: an empirical analysis of process development', *Strategic Management Journal*, 15: 85–100.

Pucik, V. (1988) 'Strategic alliances, organizational learning, and competitive advantage: the HRM agenda', *Human Resource Management*, 27: 77–93.

Purser, R. and Pasmore, W. (1992) 'Organizing for learning', in Pasmore, W.A. and Wooodman, R.W. (eds), *Research in Organizational Change and Development*, 6th edn, JAI Press, Greenwich, CT, pp. 37–114.

Pye, A. (1994) 'Past, present and possibility: an integrative appreciation of learning from experience', *Management Learning*, 25: 155–73.

Quinn, J. (1992) *The Intelligent Enterprise: A New Paradigm*, Free Press, New York.

Reinhardt, R. (1993) *Das Modell Organisationaler lernfähigkeit und die Gestaltung lernfähiger Organisationen*, Peter Lang, Frankfurt.

Rieckmann, H. and Sievers, B. (1978) 'Lernende Organisation — Organisiertes Lernen. Systemveränderung und Lernen in sozialen Organisationen', in Bartölke and Kappler (eds), *Arbeitsqualität in Organisation*, Gabler, Wiesbaden, pp. 259–77.

Roth, A., Marucheck, A., Kemp, A. and Trimble, D. (1994) 'The knowledge factory for accelerated learning practices', *Planning Review*, 22: 26–32.

Schein, E. (1993) 'How can organizations learn faster? The challenge of entering the green room', *Sloan Management Review*, 34: 85–92.

Senge, P. (1991) 'Learning organizations', *Executive Excellence*, 8: 7–8.

Senge, P. (1991) 'The learning organization made plain', *Training and Development*, October, 37–44.

Senge, P. (1992) 'Mental models', *Planning Review*, 20: 4–10.

Senge, P. and Fulmer, R. (1993) 'Simulations, systems thinking and anticipatory learning', *Journal of Management Development*, 12: 21–33.

Senge, P., Meen, D. and Keough, M. (1992) 'Creating the learning organization', *The McKinsey Quarterly*, 1: 58–77.

Senge, P., Kleiner, A., Roberts, C., Ross, R. and Smith, B. (1994) *The Fifth Discipline Book: Strategies and Tools for Building a Learning Organization*, Doubleday, New York.

Simon, H.A. (1991) 'Bounded rationality and organizational learning', *Organization Science*, 2(1): 125–34.

Simonin, B. and Helleloid, D. (1993) 'Do organizations learn? An empirical test of organizational learning in international strategic alliances', *Academy of Management Proceedings, 1993*.

Simonin, B. and Helleloid, D. (1993) 'An Empirical Investigation of Double-loop Learning in International Collaborations', Working Paper, University of Washington, Seattle.

Sinulka, J. (1994) 'Market information processing and organizational learning', *Journal of Marketing*, **58**: 35–45.

Sitkin, S. (1992) 'Learning through alliances: the strategy of small losses', *Research in Organizational Behavior*, **14**: 231–66.

Slepian, J. (1993) 'Learning, belief and action in organizational work groups: a conceptual model of work group learning', Working Paper, Academy of Management, Atlanta.

Slocum, J., McGill, M. and Lei, D. (1994) 'The new learning strategy: anytime, anything, anywhere', *Organizational Dynamics*, **23**: 33–47.

Spender, J-C. (1993) 'Competitive advantage from tacit knowledge? Unpacking the concept and its strategic implications', *Academy of Management Proceedings, 1993*.

Starbuck, W. (1992) 'Learning by knowledge-intensive firms', *Journal of Management Studies*, **29**: 713–40.

Stata, R. (1989) 'Organizational learning: the key to management innovation', *Sloan Management Review*, **30**: 63–74.

Stata, R. (1992) 'Organizational learning in practice', *McKinsey Quarterly*, **1**: 79–82.

Stata, R. (1992) 'Organizational learning: the key to success in the 1990s', *Prism*, **4**: 87–104.

Thurbin, P. (1994) *Implementing the Learning Organisation*, Pitman, London.

Torbert, W. (1994) 'Managerial learning, organizational learning: a potentially powerful redundancy', *Management Learning*, **25**: 57–70.

Useem, M. and Kochan, T.A. (1992) 'Creating the learning organization', in Kochan, T. and Useem, M. (eds), *Transforming Organizations*, Oxford University Press, New York, pp. 393–406.

Van de Ven, A. and Polley, D. (1992) 'Learning while innovating', *Organization Science*, **3**: 92–116.

Van Wart, M. (1994) 'Learning and the reinvention of public sector organizations', *Public Administration Review*, **54**: 577–9.

Watkins, K. and Marsick, V. (1993) *Sculpting the Learning Organization*, Jossey-Bass, San Francisco.

Weick, K. (1991) 'The nontraditional quality of organizational learning', *Organization Science*, **2**(1): 116–24.

Wick, C. and Leon, S. (1995) 'From ideas to action: creating a learning organization', *Human Resource Management*, **34**: 299–311.

Wolff, R. (1982) *Der Prozess des Organisierens: Zu einer Theorie des organisationellen Lernens*, Wilfer, Spardorf.

Young, D., Pieters, G. and Cherin, D. (1994) 'Building centers for learning', *Human Resources Professional*, **7**: 10–14.

Index

Aare-Emmenkanal Ltd 162
ability 170, 171
acquisitions 3, 122
adaptive learning 32–3
agents 55–62, 80, 81
alliances 3, 123–5, 148, 149–50
Allianz Insurance 60–2
ascom 124
Asea Brown Boveri (ABB) 6, 9, 10–11, 38–9,
    48, 143–4, 159–61
assumptions, analysis 139–41
Austrian Airlines 125
autonomy 127, 128
axiomatic knowledge 24

British Aerospace plc 156–7

capacity for action 9, 16
Challenger disaster 73–4
Ciba-Geigy 131–3
classical learning theory 14
coaching 148, 149–50
coalition 116, 119
cognitive approach 14
cognitive distortions 159, 160
cognitive maps 24, 35, 103, 148, 159, 160
cognitive patterns 24
collective thinking 18
collective writing 164–5
communication fora 138–41
communications 19, 19–20, 21 *Fig*, 56, 138–41,
    168–9
company climate 141–6
competitive pressure 3, 45
competitiveness, significance of delays 5 *Fig*
complexity 4
computer simulated microworlds 89–95

conceptual maps 157
conflicts 45, 125, 128
cooperation 3
cooperative arrangements 122–8
    see also alliances; joint ventures
core groups 150
crisis 6, 44–5
culture 9, 21, 60, 69, 85, 128
    development 85, 129–46
        vision and mission statements 129–37
Customer Focus 143
customer orientation 40–1
customer satisfaction 41, 142–4

decision-making by interdisciplinary
        groups 17, 18 *Fig*
defensive patterns 35, 66–70, 73–4
development alliances 148, 149–50
dictionary knowledge 23
Digital Equipment Corporation 9, 40–1, 150
Digital Equipment Enterprise 126–8
directory knowledge 23
diversity 19
double-loop learning 34
Dutch Petroleum 102–3

early warning indicators 46, 50–2, 103, 105,
    142
electricity and gas industries, cooperation 3
elites 57, 81
employee dissatisfaction 45
employee motivation 144
entrepreneurs 40–1
espoused theories 22, 24
ethics 6
European Quality Alliance (EQA) 125
experimentation 95

fancy footwork 69, 70
feedback 146, 153
flexibility 4, 127, 128
flexible team 110
fluid hierarchies 28, 110
Forbo International 119–20
force field analysis 75–7, 81
frame of reference 21, 22, 34, 139

games 88–95
globalization 3, 10–11
goals 21, 22, 27–8, 127–8, 144
Gore & Associates Inc 137–8
groups 57–8, 60–2, 81, 147
growth 2, 3–4

heterarchy 29, 117–19
Hewlett-Packard 9, 46, 49–52, 143, 144–6
hierarchies, fluid 28, 110
Hoffman–La Roche 162–5
Honda 119
human resources 85
  development 85, 147–65
  development alliances 149–50
  policy 38–9

IBM 9, 48–9
identity 27
image, barometer 51–2, 142, 144
image analysis 142–6
individual learning 14, 15–20, 55–6, 148
information, open provision 35
information disorders 71–2
information processing capacity 71–2
innovation cycles, shortening 6
instruction 149
instruments, strategic 88
integrated network thinking 98–9, 100
integration 19, 20, 21 *Fig*, 127
intention 170
interdisciplinary databank 120
interventions, on-the-job 151–7

Jakob Schläpfer Ltd 26–9
joint ventures 3, 123

knowledge 16, 167–8, 170
  criteria for determining 172
  growth 4–5
  shared 19, 23–4, 128, 164
  store of 20, 80
knowledge assets 79
knowledge structures, development 23
Kuoni Travel Group 98–102, 143

leadership 21, 47–8, 127, 128, 132
learning
  ability 168–9

adaptive 32–3
agents 55–62, 80
barriers 64–74, 167
  defensive patterns 66–70, 74
  information disorders 71–2
  norms, privileges and taboos 70–1
  overcoming 58
definitions 166–7
elites 57
facilitation 78–86
forms of 79, 80
groups 57–8, 60–2
individual 14, 55–6, 148
  compared with organizational 15–20
instruments 146, 168, 170, 171, 172
level of 32–7, 60, 80
need for 9, 79, 80
obstacles 47
profile 78–81
readiness for 110, 114
reconstructive 33–5
social systems 58–60
see also organizational learning
learning conceptions, overview 25 *Fig*
learning cycles, unlearning 35
learning partnerships 148–50
learning process 35–7, 41, 167
  initiation 81, 84–6
learning-oriented projects 152–4

McDonalds 121–2
magic square 84–5
malaise 69, 70
management by objectives (MBO) 167
maps 157–65
  conceptual 157
market launch, importance of timing 6, 7 *Fig*
maturity of organization 169–73
measurement systems 105–7
mental plans 24
mentoring 148, 149, 150
mergers 3
microworlds, computer simulated 89–95
mind-mapping 159–61, 162, 163

network organizations 116–22
network structures 40–1
network thinking 50–1
networks 116–17
norms 70

officially espoused theories 22, 29
organizational defensive routines 35, 69, 151
organizational learning
  definition 15, 167
  importance 1–11
  nature 32–41
  recognizing 23–4

transformational conditions   19, 20 *Fig*
  see also learning
Oticon   48
Oticon Holding A/S   154–6

paper, elimination of   156
parallel organizations   110
patterns, cognitive   24
pay and incentives   151
perception   23
perceptual filter   139
personnel policy   38–9
planning seminar, use of microworld   93–5
power relations   21
privileges   71
proactive attitude   9
problem-solving   17
process learning   35–7, 41
process orientation   168
projects   109–15
  learning-oriented   152–4
  management   110–13
  teams   110, 112, 153–5
  work   151

re-engineering   46
reality, views of   19, 94
recipe knowledge   24
reconstructive learning   33–5, 39, 41
redimensioning   3, 4
redundancy   46, 47, 127
reflection   36
reframing   35
restructuring   46
rotation principle   151
routines
  defensive   35, 66–70, 73–4
  organizational defensive   35, 69, 151
Royal Dutch Petroleum/Shell   102–3

SAS   125
scenario technique   88, 95–103
scenarios   95, 96–8
Schäpfer Emroideries   119
schemata   24
shadow economy   68
shared vision   130
Shell   102–3
simulation games   88–95

single-loop learning   33
Skandia AFS   105–7
skilled incompetence   67–8, 69
slack   46–7
social systems   58–60
speed of change   95
standard of living 1900–2100   2
storage systems   55, 58–60
strategy   21, 85, 162
  control   88, 103–7
  development process   85, 87–107
  strategic alliances   3, 123–5
  strategic instruments   88
  strategic planning   87–8
stress   45
structural development   85, 108–28
structural networks, characteristics   116
structure   21, 85
suggestions and innovations, channel for   151
supply management   11
Swissair   111, 125
Swisscontrol   133–7

taboos   71
'Tanaland' computer simulation   90–3
terminology, classification   37 *Fig*
theories
  of action   20–3
  official   22, 29
theories in use   22–3, 24, 29
time, importance   5–6, 7
time-based management (TBM)   11
total quality management (TQM)   11, 167
transparency   19, 20, 21 *Fig*, 168
triggers   44–51, 80, 81, 88

unlearning   64–5
  definition   64

values, change in   6–9
views of reality   19, 94
vision and mission statements   21, 129–37, 162
Volkswagen Ltd   140–1

will to learn   169, 172
Winterthur Insurance   113–15
workgroups   60–2
workshops   29, 103, 114, 162